NO ACCIDENTAL MISSIONARY

How an Ethiopian man became a Christian in Saudi Arabia, and a missionary to America. The Biography of Tesfai Tesema

Marilyn Feldhaus

NO ACCIDENTAL MISSIONARY
© 2018 Mission Nation Publishing

ISBN: 0996677968
ISBN: 13: 9780996677967

Dedicated to David, with deepest gratitude and love; and with thanks to Tesfai for all the espressos.

ABOUT THE AUTHOR

Marilyn is a retired special education teacher who - when she is not writing for Mission Nation Publishing - enjoys hiking, volunteering, cooking, choral singing and playing piano. She lives with her husband in San Jose, California.

A WORD FROM THE PUBLISHER

I did not know Tesfai Tesema before this book was begun. I had heard about him, though, from Ethiopian and Eritrean friends. They had been impressed at how strategic he had been in starting a new mission among Ethiopian immigrants in northern California. Tesfai is well known in the large Ethiopian network in the United States, and travels still to Ethiopia as a resource for outreach and church planting. He focuses his life in America on the families of immigrants, finding what is needed to support their need to feel settled in a strange new land.

I learned later that Tesfai had been born into an Orthodox Christian family, but the faith never "took." As a teenager he used drugs and generally lived a life of a pagan. As a young adult he became attracted to the communism practiced by some Ethiopians – he admired the Communist concern for the poor. Tesfai broke whatever ties he still had with Christianity, and became a member of the communist party, and was given a job in the communist government of Ethiopia, until he fell into disfavor. I learned that later on he became a Christian in Saudi Arabia.

How could that be? Why did he come to faith in Jesus? That is what this book is about.

Robert Scudieri
Publisher, Mission Nation Publishing

THE CONTRIBUTED TO THE PUBLICATION OF THIS BOOK,
FOR WHICH WE ARE MOST GRATEFUL:

<u>Senior Publisher</u>
Peace Lutheran Church, Naples, Florida. Pr. Karl Galik

<u>Publishers</u>
Sara Agee
Alison Greenhill
Prof. Andrew Bartelt
Carol and Dr. Alan Buckman
Dr. Yared Halche
Yvonne Gurnee
Colonel Jim Schlie
John and Linda Friend
Dr. Yohannes Mengsteab
Keith and Sandra Gollenberg
Bob and Lynn Scudieri

TABLE OF CONTENTS

NO ACCIDENTAL MISSIONARY

If someone had told young Tesfai Tesema, seated alongside his drinking buddies at a bar in Addis Ababa, that one day he would become a Christian missionary to America, a dedicated "fool for Christ," he would have laughed out loud.

But just a few months later found Tesfai and two of his companions alone in the Danakil desert, abandoned by their guides. All they had was the small amount of water and food they'd placed by their sleeping places in the cool desert evening the night before. No one heard the guides leave, and soon the deadly heat would arrive.

Now Tesfai remembered the foreboding feeling he'd had earlier, when the guides had suggested—demanded, really—that he and the young women with him hand over their money and documents, "For safekeeping," Abdul and Mohammed had said.

They were going to have to figure out how to survive, alone, without a map, or a compass, or supplies in the bleak desert. The Danakil, he knew, was tens of thousands of square miles of unforgiving territory: filled with hazards—including nomadic tribes sure to be hostile to obvious city dwellers such as himself and the two young women with him.

Tesfai went to wake his companions. Their journey to Djibouti had just become even more dangerous. What he could not know was that this was no accident. It was the beginning of a journey that had been planned for him from the beginning.

To understand that plan, it is necessary to begin the account a few years before.

A FATHER'S INCREDULITY

"You want to do what?" Zeleke Tesema stared at his son. Rubbing his forehead with his thumb and fingers, he sighed wearily. "Just why do you propose to go to Germany? After all you've put your mother and me through, why would I consider such a request?"

Tesfai answered carefully. "Germany could be a new start for me. I'd learn German, go to school, I'd ..."

His father erupted. "Go to school! You didn't think school was important here in Ethiopia. You cut classes; you flunked out; when you did graduate, your grades were so poor you couldn't get accepted into university. Any university, anywhere here in our country! And now you say you'll be disciplined enough to learn German and go to school in Germany? I don't believe it!"

Tesfai averted his eyes. "I know I've been a disappointment, but I can change. They do things differently in Germany, and I wouldn't have so many friends around. Maybe my friends are a bad influence on me."

"Tesfai, you have a gift for making friends and then everyone seems to end up in bars and juke joints instead of, say, in school. You think I don't know that? And by the way, I also know about the beer halls in Germany!" Tesfai's father glared at his son. "I don't believe your friends are the bad influence; I think you're just as eager as they to get into trouble."

"So, father, consider this. Germany has a different form of government than we do in Ethiopia. It's a democracy; Ethiopia has an emperor with absolute rule and you know from experience his power to help or hinder."

"Indeed I do. That reminds me of another failure of yours: the commission I secured—at considerable financial expense to myself— from Emperor Haile Selassie so you could be an officer in his military. Not an enlisted man, an officer. A safe job, a good job! And you lasted three months! Too much discipline, you complained. And now you tell me that you will be disciplined in Germany? What kind of a fool do you think I am?"

"Dad, I'm older now. I know I've not obeyed you. I didn't do well in school here. I wasn't cut out for military life. Believe it or not, I actually do want to be useful. I've heard about how in Germany the government will help with language classes and expenses. I can be a guest worker. It's a new environment, and I need a second chance."

Tesfai rested his case and waited silently.

His father, too, was pensive. Finally, he murmured to himself. "Maybe it's for the best. The Emperor's reign is becoming tenuous. Communists are marching in the streets. People are restless, and there are rumors of a revolution. Who knows what Ethiopia will be like in a few months or even weeks?" He looked at his son. "You may go. I'm not happy, but you may go. All I ask is that you manage to stay out of trouble."

Tesfai knew better than to make promises, having broken so many others. He also knew better than to mention he'd been part of those Communist demonstrations his father abhorred.

"And now …" Tesfai's father stood. "I need to tell your mother. She may welcome the news."

4

A NEW START FOLLOWING
THE LAST NEW START

Tesfai Tesema, Zeleke Tesema, and Mebrat Hailu sat on the verandah of their Addis Ababa home, glumly drinking their afternoon coffee. The coffee, thick and aromatic, brewed slowly from Ethiopian grown coffee beans, was delicious. The gathering was anything but. Tesfai's father had called this meeting. Tesfai's mother had insisted on joining the conversation. All were contemplating Tesfai's abrupt return from Germany the day before.

"I see you were no more successful in Germany than you had been here." Tesfai knew better than to protest. Mebrat stared at her coffee.

"Give me those papers you brought from the German authorities. I want to know how my eldest son, my first-born child, should have failed in Germany, especially after he assured me he would go to classes and learn a trade!" Zeleke reached out his hand. Tesfai relinquished the incriminating German reports. As Tesfai translated the reports for his father, Zeleke grew increasingly agitated.

Tesfai's father summarized what he'd heard. "Enrolled for German government support, yes, you did that. Signed up for German classes, yes, you did that too. Ah, an attendance summary—it only took a few weeks for you to decide you didn't need to learn German? This summary says you had more 'absents' than 'presents.' And what were you doing instead, since without knowing German you couldn't work?"

Tesfai remained silent. "Citations for unruly conduct. One, no two, no three, for public drunkenness. One for loitering. Warnings about skipping class. More warnings. Revocation of government support; something about you being a drain on German society." Mr. Tesema stared at the papers on the table and stared at his son. "You are an embarrassment to me and your mother. I've a mind to kick you out of my house! You are useless!"

Zeleke paused. "Not only are you useless, you have terrible timing! People are desperately trying to get out of Ethiopia, and you get yourself forced back into Ethiopia. Our family could have used your success in Germany, if only you'd been responsible enough to be successful!"

While Tesfai was in Germany, the military coup his father feared had taken place. Emperor Haile Selassie—Ethiopia's longtime monarch and often grantor of favors to Tesfai's father—was deposed and living in exile. The new rulers were Colonel Mengistu Haile Mariam and his military Derg. They were brutal replacements.

In 1974, while the Cold War between Western nations and the Soviet Union was still raging across the world, especially in Africa, the pro-Western Haile Selassie had been supplanted by the pro-Soviet Communist Derg. The Derg did not recognize private property, which Zeleke Tesema had accumulated. Mr. Tesema was also guilty of having served for many years in the Emperor's military.

Zeleke gave Tesfai his frank assessment. "I can no longer support you. I am under a cloud with this new government, and my lands and money are being expropriated. I don't know how you're going to do this, useless as you have been, but you must start pulling your own weight!" He leaned back: his eyes narrow, his mouth a tight line, and glared at his son.

Tesfai's mother spoke. Father and son had almost forgotten she was present. "I think I can help. Zeleke, of course, with your family's military service and ties to Emperor Selassie we are not considered loyal. But my side of the family had no connections to the Emperor. I have a second cousin who got a job working for this new government. I will contact my cousin, Berhane. I am sure he can find a position working for the Derg. Tesfai, when this job comes, you must take it. Do it, my son, for me, if for no other reason!" Mebrat's eyes blazed as she entreated Tesfai.

Tesfai and Zeleke turned to face her, one in hope, the other in resignation. For Tesfai, this entreaty from his mother was an opportunity to avoid his father's disapproval and garner yet another chance.

Zeleke sighed. "Tesfai, when you weren't fooling around in high school, you were spouting all that Marxist nonsense you learned on those days you actually attended school. Yes, I know your teachers loved Communism and so do you. You might as well get paid by these Communists, since they're now in charge and busily taking my property away. Do as your mother says: take the job!"

With that, Zeleke stalked into the house. Mebrat breathed a sigh of relief. Tesfai, who was indeed enamored with Communism, agreed to work for the Communist Derg. How hard could it be?

A HASTY DEPARTURE

Tesfai approached the Megala Bar in central Metehara. He'd finished his hour-long bus ride from Awara Melka, where he was assigned to the Ministry of Agriculture and Resettlement. The department was a new creation of the Derg government. This morning Tesfai had an appointment with Mehari, his superior officer and co-conspirator; the usual place for their frequent meetings was this bar on the main square.

The area could be counted on for bustling activity, chaotic crowds and dust kicked up by cars, buses and vendors' wagons. It was the perfect place for a clandestine meeting. The loud music coming from the jukebox hindered eavesdropping.

Instead of the usual coded greetings, when he spotted Tesfai Mehari simply exclaimed "Tesfai! We need to get out of here! Now!"

Tesfai drew back. "Why, what's happened?" He glanced around quickly, taking in the other dozen or so bar patrons.

Furtively, Mehari whispered, "They're on to you! They went to Awara Melka to take you into custody, and it won't be long before they return. We've got to get out of here now!" Mehari looked from side to side. "We've got to get to Addis Ababa, and in a big hurry, before they give our names to any of the checkpoints!"

"You are also a suspect?" Tesfai tried to process the news.

"Indeed, I am, or I will be, once they get all their informants together." Mehari fumbled with the documents in his hand, collected hastily from his office.

"The bus for Addis is arriving now." Tesfai nodded toward the bus stop across the town square.

"Let's grab it. Run! We can't miss it! We need to stay ahead of them!"

The men dashed for the bus stop where the gray commuter bus was just pulling up. Called a leonchena, it was one of the frequent workhorse buses traveling to Addis Ababa. The men managed to scramble up its steep steps seconds before it lurched away from the stop. They settled into a vacant seat to endure the five-hour journey. It was a trip punctuated by heat, many stops, and checkpoints set up unpredictably along the way.

They could only hope they would escape detection.

They agreed that if they arrived safely in Addis Ababa, they would separate and hide among Addis's larger population. Mehari voiced what Tesfai already knew. "If they arrest us, first they'll torture us. Then they'll kill us."

Tesfai needed no explanation. "They" were the Derg. Tesfai reflected how he now found himself on the Derg's hit list. It almost made him smile, despite his fear. His mind turned to when he had started his most recent job with the Derg.

"Ah, the new man, Comrade Tesfai Tesema!" Mehari had greeted him upon his arrival in Metehara a couple of years earlier. "You come to us well recommended from the work you did with the farmers in Gondar."

Tesfai nodded. His first job, in Gondar province, had been to promote socialist land ownership among the peasants, converting farm workers into landowners on behalf of "the people." In line with the Derg's Marxist ideology and his inclinations, Tesfai had thrown himself into the work with gusto; he was eager to overturn Emperor Selassie's feudal system of land ownership in favor of the Derg's land-reform goals. The Derg came to power vowing to re-distribute land so more people would become land owners. To ac-complish this, land was expropriated from rich landlords, most of whom had owned the land for generations.

Tesfai's job was to help farm workers gain the skills to be suc-cessful landowners.

Mehari continued, "Your previous colleagues say you easily make friends with just about anyone. A talent we can use."

Tesfai smiled. His father had often complained about this characteristic.

Zeleke had not seen it as a talent.

Then Mehari leaned in. He said quietly, "I have heard rumors that you are a true believer in Communism. If so, maybe you can help bring true socialism to Ethiopia."

Tesfai inclined his head, indicating he understood. His new boss was, like him, a Derg government employee, but he was also a clandestine member of the "socialist opposition" known as the EPRP: the Ethiopian People's Revolutionary Party. The Derg was modeled after Russian communism; the EPRP was a follower of the Chinese model.

"The Derg has betrayed the people," whispered Mehari. "We need to get back to revolutionary principles and help the people. Will you join us?"

Tesfai agreed. "I've seen that Derg officials only care about wealth and privilege, just like the Emperor's people did. This is not the Marxism I learned about!"

"It will be dangerous."

Tesfai had accepted the challenge. He began living a double life, opposing the government while he continued working for the Derg in Awara Melka. As the bus lumbered along, he recalled this job that had introduced him to Mehari and the EPRP.

He'd been working among Afar nomads. The Derg's goal was to convert the Afar people from herders to settled farmers. Besides various food crops, cash crops such as cotton were encouraged. However, everything grown ended up being appropriated by the Derg to forward its goals; the people were not better off. Tesfai had found the arrangement offensive; the Derg showed a disregard for socialist principles and a lack of concern for the people's wellbeing.

Tesfai's thoughts brought him back to late-night meetings of EPRP members, his fervor in pursuing a government that would help all Ethiopia's people, and the increasingly violent conflicts between Derg and EPRP operatives. While he was never involved in the violence, he realized it would only be a matter of time before the Derg would quit making a distinction between fighters and sympathizers.

Then, in 1978, the Derg instituted its Red Terror. No longer pretending to be the Communist party of the people, the Derg was intent on wiping out any opposition to its repressive military rule. Tesfai, age 23, was now a target of the Red Terror. He was on the run; he had to stay hidden.

The bus wheezed along. The tan, dusty sprawl of Addis Ababa loomed in the distance. Tesfai prepared himself to go into hiding.

TROUBLE AT THE TRIANO

The day started out like all the others since Tesfai's return to Addis Ababa. After parting from Mehari, Tesfai had done his best to stay undetected. He'd moved from safe house to safe house while avoiding his parents' home. He'd been diligent about varying his travels in the large, dusty city.

However, Tesfai was consistent about meeting his high school buddies each day at the Triano Coffee Bar. Located off one of the busier side streets near Addis Ababa's Piazza, the Triano was a favorite for its macchiato, its beer, its access to marijuana, and its billiards-playing patrons. Tesfai had observed that the neighborhood's residents were occupied with their own concerns.

Unlike the people swarming around him, he had no sidewalk stall, no street cleaning, no bicycle or cart for hauling produce or messages, no briefcase or other parcels in his hands. Tesfai and his friends were engaged in hanging around drinking, smoking, and playing pool. Although he had gotten to recognize some of the local residents and their routines, he felt he was invisible. He liked that feeling.

But today, as Tesfai approached the Triano, he sensed a change in the mood. Curious, wary glances seemed to follow him as he ambled along the sidewalk. People seemed to step out of his way instead of the usual jostling.

Tesfai was aware that the Derg had begun another wave of persecution of its enemies in the Ethiopian People's Revolutionary Party, but surely a few young guys playing pool would escape suspicion. But then, why did today's street activity seem so subdued—or was it his imagination?

Tesfai reached the Triano and entered. Inside, along with one of his friends, he was greeted by two men wearing the uniform of the Derg Revolutionary Guards. A third man, another Guard, moved from the bar's shadowy wall to block the door. "We don't know exactly who you are, but you two are under arrest."

Tesfai could feel color draining from his face. "On what charge?"

"Loitering with no social purpose. The neighbors have noticed you have no job, no visible means of support, but each day, here you are playing pool and smoking and drinking."

Tesfai was silent.

"We are taking you into custody as enemies of the state. Perhaps you can be rehabilitated into useful members of our great socialist society. But if not ..." The Guard let the sentence go unfinished.

They had no choice but to accompany the three men into a black van. Tesfai and his friend were shoved into the van's back seat and wedged between two Guards while the third Guard joined the driver in front.

Tesfai could only guess how much danger he was in. Had the Guards really arrested him for "loitering" or did they know he was in the EPRP? Were they waiting for him to contradict himself during interrogation? Would he ever see his family again? Would he end up like so many other "enemies of the state," a mutilated corpse by the side of some road?

Finally, the van pulled into the courtyard of a foreboding brick building, clearly a prison. Tesfai recognized it as the place where political prisoners and others in need of "rehabilitation" were sent. He knew not all prisoners came out alive.

As he was hustled along a dark corridor toward a waiting prison cell, Tesfai could hear men screaming. Unbeliever though he was, he could not help but plead, "Dear God, help me!"

When the cell door slammed behind Tesfai, he was alone with his fears.

PRAYERS AND LUCK

Tesfai's father heard the knock on the front door. For Ethiopians in 1979, a knock at the door could signal anything, from a neighbor wanting to visit over coffee to a raid by the Derg.

Zeleke was apprehensive. He had lost his money and his land, and now his son Tesfai was in prison. Ever since Tesfai's arrest three months earlier, the government had stayed silent regarding his fate. Glancing at his wife, Zeleke edged toward the gate.

"Yes?" called Mr. Tesema. "Who is there?"

"Father," came the soft reply. "It's me: Tesfai!"

Zeleke threw open the door, grabbed his son by the arm, and dragged him inside. He quickly shut the gate.

"Tesfai! Tesfai, you're here! Mebrat, it's Tesfai!"

Mebrat rushed past her husband to hug their son, tears running down her cheeks. "My son! You're here! God has answered our prayers: you are alive!"

"We never lost hope." Zeleke was stammering. "But after three months, we were fearing the worst."

"As was I, father. But not only have I been released, I have a letter. It's from the arresting authorities. It's addressed to my work place, saying I was in prison, but now I have been cleared to work."

"How is that possible?" Zeleke was skeptical. "I mean, we are grateful, but since when has the Derg become merciful to dissidents?" Zeleke and Mebrat steered their son to a seat on the verandah, waiting to hear about this miracle.

"Well, the good news is that while the Derg may be vicious, it is not all knowing. You call it prayer, I call it a lot of luck. The authorities who arrested me had no idea about my work in Metehara, or that I was wanted there. They only arrested me because I was loitering, drinking, and playing pool."

"And you kept your mouth shut," guessed Zeleke.

"I kept my mouth shut, and played along" agreed Tesfai. "I let them believe I was a no-good useless individual. I avoided being tortured or killed; instead, they educated me in the principles of Derg socialism, and now I have this letter to take to the head office for the Ministry of Agriculture and Resettlement, where I was previously employed by the Derg government."

"In other words, your unpleasant habits saved you." Mebrat let out a long breath. Zeleke allowed himself the faintest of smiles.

"You could say that. Meanwhile, word got around the prison that the Derg was going crazy, rounding up political dissidents outside wherever they could find them. But since I was already in jail, they did not find me. My jailers did not know I was wanted for my political activities. The Derg's secret police did not know I was in jail. I got to hide from the Derg by getting a socialist education."

Zeleke spoke. "My son, for once I am glad about your aimless lifestyle."

He went on. "But now, what will you do?"

"I must go to the headquarters of the Ministry of Agriculture and Resettlement and officially get my assignment to the town of Welkite, which I requested," Tesfai answered.

"Welkite, that is not Metehara," mused Zeleke.

"I did not want to return to Metehara for obvious reasons. Hopefully, my assignment in Welkite will keep me safe—if I am not in Metehara they can't catch me!" explained Tesfai.

Mebrat was worried. "What if the Metehara officials communicate with the Addis headquarters about you? Wouldn't you get arrested again as soon as you go to the headquarters to get your papers?"

"It is a chance I have to take, as it is likely the prison has already told the headquarters to expect me. I'm guessing if the jail and the headquarters in Addis don't talk to each other, maybe there is also no talking between Metehara and Addis. Anyway, I need to go, but I must go immediately so I can get out of town before anyone realizes there has been a mistake."

"You don't worry they may eventually catch up with you in Welkite?" asked Tesfai's father.

"I have to take the chance. It's a three-hour drive to Welkite, and a bus would take even longer. I am not the most important dissident out there, which might help protect me. Now that I have this paper they might even decide I am no longer a threat. I'm not sure how safe I am, but this is my best option for now."

"What strange times we live in," sighed Zeleke. He stood. "Go with my blessing."

"And stay alive!" added Mebrat.

QUESTIONS IN WELKITE

Much to his parents' relief, Tesfai's visit to the Derg's Ministry of Agriculture and Resettlement headquarters was successful. He began his job in Welkite as an assistant administrator, organizing the resettlement and farming project in the town.

According to Derg propaganda, this collectivizing and mechanizing agriculture would make farming more efficient and make Ethiopia self- sufficient in food production. As he settled into his organizing work, Tesfai found himself in conversation with his boss, also new to Welkite, who oversaw farming operations.

Tesfai would organize the farmers. "I understand about the organizing part, but I am wondering how this will grow more food."

"Instead of lots of little farms growing whatever they want, we'll educate the farmers to what Ethiopia needs! And, with the larger farms, we can supply the seeds and the equipment and the transport for what is grown. We'll have the farmers live together and work together and then we will have more land for farming!"

Tesfai's body tensed. He had spent a lot of time talking to the farmers; they were anxious about the new system. "But many of these farm workers are not from here. They've been relocated from elsewhere. Some of the new people have never even farmed before. How will they adjust to this new life?" Tesfai was thankful he and his boss had developed a respectful relationship. He was asking sensitive questions.

"This is for the good of Ethiopia. More land under cultivation, lots of trained farmers, more food production. Besides, less land will be used for small houses in the middle of inefficient small farms."

"Okay," said Tesfai. "Mechanized farming, communal living. But then the farmers must travel further, to land they don't own, to grow food.

And then?"

"The people in charge have figured this all out. They're following the model of the Soviet Union, which has been successfully collectivizing for decades. Don't forget that!"

"But the farmers have asked about the government's plan to buy their produce for low prices. Many of them are used to higher prices. Will this really help?"

"I think you are asking the wrong question," responded Tesfai's boss. "The real question is, how will this help Ethiopia? We know rural people in Ethiopia are uneducated, and backward; they need guidance. Left on their own, they will only do what is good for themselves. But we are building a self-sufficient Ethiopia. To do that we must help the people realize their concerns are small compared to what they can do for the country.

Ethiopia has city people who need food; the government needs money for programs. Collective, mechanized farming can provide both—food for the population and cash crops the government can sell to raise money. We have to organize them to meet these goals!"

"But what about rainfall? We cannot count on good rains. What if the rains fail and we have all these people dependent on one way of farming? And when they grow food, and we don't pay a good price for what we take, won't that mean the farmers won't want to work so hard? I'm just wondering." Tesfai added the last bit hastily.

"Ah, Tesfai. You ask too many questions. This can cause problems. We need to trust our leaders; that is why they are our leaders. And we need to help our rural people understand their important role in making a great Ethiopia! I like you, Tesfai. You have a good way with these farmers. But remember, it is not about us or the farmers, it is about the Derg's plan to make Ethiopia great! Collective farming is the way for the farmers to help."

Tesfai, in the months following, tried to set aside his concerns as he carried out his organizing work. He accepted the idealism of his boss.

Then, one morning, he got an urgent phone summons to visit his parents in Addis Ababa. When he arrived, they had news that would haunt Tesfai for the rest of his life.

TERRIBLE NEWS

"Your brother, Yosef, is dead!"

Tesfai had barely had a chance to greet his parents when Mebrat blurted out the news. "Yosef? How can it be?" Tesfai grasped the nearest wall to keep himself from collapsing. "He was the talented one! What happened?"

"Like you, your brother was involved in the underground opposition to the regime," explained his father. "Unlike you, he had always wanted to be a soldier and, as you know, passed the exams to be an officer. Then, when the Derg came to power, he found himself trying to be a good army officer while also being part of the political opposition,"

"You had to buy me a commission in the army. But Yosef became a cadet on his own, and when he was only sixteen! I admired him so much!

My younger brother dead, I can't believe it!"

"Yosef's goal was to become a general," resumed Zeleke. "He was even willing to serve in the Derg's army. But then he couldn't take the Derg's oppression of our people, and their using the army as an instrument of that oppression!"

"So, like me, he joined the EPRP ..."

Zeleke nodded despondently, "Yes, Yosef joined the EPRP. We argued about it. In my opinion, both Derg and EPRP are equally responsible for the political violence in our country. Yosef disagreed; he felt he had to join the EPRP to get rid of the Derg,".

"And he got caught?" Tesfai sank into a chair, his head in his hands.

"He got caught," confirmed Zeleke. "The Derg infiltrated Yosef's network and came to arrest him. Your brother died in a shoot-out during the arrest."

Now the mother spoke. "Tesfai, Yosef has been taken away from us. But I keep thinking, if they could kill Yosef, they can kill you too! How long will it take for them to find you, Yosef's brother? And to figure out your history? You have been lucky so far."

Mebrat, Zeleke and Tesfai fell silent until at last Mebrat spoke again. "Tesfai, you must leave Ethiopia. You can figure it out with your father, but you must leave! Your father and I cannot lose another son!"

Tesfai responded carefully. "I agree with you; the time has come. I dare not mention Yosef's death to my boss. I'll return to work and arrange to come home again quickly. I have vacation time. I'll use that time to leave Ethiopia. By the time my vacation days are over and I'm expected back at work, I will be out of the country."

Tesfai's father concurred. "You have been living on borrowed time. We must act before ..."

"I too wind up dead," finished Tesfai. "It is time for me to escape east to Djibouti."

MAKING TRAVEL PLANS

Tesfai and his father knew getting to Djibouti wasn't as easy as taking a train or a bus. Between Addis and the nearest Djibouti town lay a few hundred miles of forbidding desert, multiple tribes with different languages, roving gangs of rebels, and Derg soldiers. Tesfai would need a local guide, someone who could navigate both territory and culture.

"My contacts say we should take a train east to Diredawa," advised Tesfai's father. "From there we can find guides to take you further east across the desert and arrange transport. They say you will likely be walking. They assure me that since Diredawa is a big trading town with merchants going constantly between Diredawa and Djibouti, you will be able to find experienced guides."

Tesfai agreed. "Father, believe it or not, my friend Abdul has already made it to Djibouti. You remember Abdul?"

"Your drinking buddy." Zeleke remembered Tesfai's friend and companion in skipping high school classes. "Why did he go to Djibouti?

Surely drinking is not on the Derg's list of crimes against the state?"

"Abdul was arrested with me, and taken to the same prison. He was released, like they released me, after they indoctrinated him with their socialist ideology. But Abdul decided he wanted nothing more to do with the Derg. Anyway, he's sent me the name of some-one in Diredawa who can help me arrange guides. So, I have a plan, if you agree. I'd rather take the train on my own; maybe this will make me less conspicuous. I'll find a group to go with me, and guides. Abdul thinks the whole trip should take only two weeks, even walking. If I move quickly, I can be in Djibouti less than three weeks from today."

"You want to go to Diredawa alone?" asked Zeleke. "What if something should go wrong? I want to go with you."

"You're needed here more. It will all be fine, I'm sure. What could possibly go wrong?"

AN UNWELCOME DISCOVERY

Tesfai awoke with a start. He was a few days into his walking journey from Diredawa to the Ethiopian border with Djibouti. He had found guides and two companions in Diredawa, two young women, Aster and Tersit. They had seen no future in Ethiopia and wanted to leave. The days had settled into a pattern of walking, resting, sleeping, and eating. The guides, while not talkative, were knowledgeable about the desert and its challenges.

However, this morning Tesfai could sense that something was wrong. It was getting toward the time when he, his female companions Aster and Tersit, and their guides Abdul and Mohammed, should be preparing for the next day of traveling east through the Danakil Desert. They were five days along in their hiking journey, with another ten yet to come.

Abdul and Mohammed should be waking them up after having returned from wherever it was they'd gone to get food and more water for the day's travel. Something was wrong. It was too quiet.

Tesfai looked about the campsite. Yes, the girls were still there, sleeping. However, he heard no sounds of the guides whispering, getting ready for another day's trek.

It was not a large campsite, but parts of their rest stop were hidden from other sections by the low bushes, the thorn trees, and taller scrub grass. So, it was not unusual that he wouldn't see the guides, as they came and went. But to not even hear them?

Tesfai went to investigate. What he found filled him with dread. Except for footprints and some beaten down grass, there was no sign of the guides. Nor of their provisions. Nor, in fact, of anything indicating the guides had any intention returning.

Tesfai and his companions were alone in the desert. All they had was the small amount of water and food they'd placed by their sleeping places in the evening.

Suddenly Tesfai remembered the foreboding feeling he'd had earlier, when the guides had suggested—demanded, really—that he and the young women hand over their money and documents needed to facilitate their way through the desert and into Djibouti. "For safekeeping," Abdul and Mohammed had said. The trio of Tesfai, Aster, and Tersit had had to comply.

Now they were going to have to figure out how to survive, alone and without essential supplies, in the desert. The Danakil, Tesfai knew, was tens of thousands of square miles of unforgiving territory: hot and frequently windy, often trackless, and filled with hazards—including nomadic groups sure to be suspicious of and hostile to obvious city dwellers such as himself and the young women.

Tesfai went to wake his companions. Their journey to Djibouti had just become even more dangerous.

DESERT DISCUSSIONS, DIRECTIONS, AND DECISIONS

When Tesfai woke the women and told them the news, they stared at him in disbelief.

Aster was the first to speak. "Oh, Tesfai; come off it! This isn't funny.

Where are they, really?"

Tersit was angry. "They can't do this. We paid them! It's not possible."

"It's possible and it's happened. We're on our own, we're lost, and we've no provisions." He added to himself, All we have are my mother's prayers, whatever good they might be doing.

The practical one, Aster, rallied them. "So, what do we do? Do we start walking? And which way?"

"We start walking," agreed Tesfai.

"Toward the railroad tracks," suggested Tersit. "Someone will come along, maybe even some police, or somebody, and help us," she added with hopeful confidence.

"I can't go that way," objected Tesfai. "I'm wanted by the government.

They find me, I'm dead."

Aster and Tersit faced him, skeptically. "Your plan is to just keep on walking? We can't find our way to safety without help, and to get help we need to find people," argued Aster.

"True enough," said Tesfai, "but I can't walk toward the railroad. Both of you are lucky enough just to be looking for a better life outside of Ethiopia. I'm looking to avoid getting caught and ending up dead. My parents have already lost one son to the Derg. I am positive they would prefer not to lose two."

Tesfai offered a small wave of his hand and began walking in the direction of the morning sun, still low enough in the east not to be unbearably hot. He knew that Djibouti was east; the sun's location was his only way of knowing which way was east.

Several minutes into his journey, he heard shouting. "Tesfai!" Aster called. "We've changed our minds! We're coming with you."

Tesfai smiled. Aster, as practical as she could be, was up for a new adventure. What better adventure than to be lost in a huge, trackless desert?

He was anxious, and wondered how far they would all get before succumbing to the desert's extreme heat. The day was just beginning when the three started walking east.

A BREAK IN THE DESERT LANDSCAPE

The three abandoned travelers walked for several hours. Their feet aching, their eyes followed the sun as it moved above them. That morning, it had started ahead of them; it was now moving to their rear. Soon, they knew, the sun would set quickly. Then they would be trading the extreme heat of the day for the equally miserable cold of the desert night.

Tersit, Aster, and Tesfai still had no real idea where they were. They were simply hoping they were closer to Djibouti than they had been.

As Tesfai surveyed the terrain, his attention was drawn to something he'd not yet seen on their trip. On the horizon, he spotted a cluster of white dwellings. Having been a government worker with the nomadic Afar people, Tesfai had enough experience to realize he was seeing nomadic homes.

He stopped walking to contemplate what to do next. It was possible the compound belonged to one of the several nomadic clans known to ply the well-known, ancient trade route between Diredawa and Djibouti. For hundreds of years groups such as these had dealt in all manner of goods and contraband between the two locales. Knowing the desert as they surely must, the clan represented by the white tents would be able to help Tesfai and his two companions get to Djibouti safely—if the clan was willing.

And that was the rub. He and the women were strangers, not just to the desert, but to the people of the desert. A man traveling with two females to whom he was not related would be antithetical to the conservative— no doubt Muslim—nomadic culture. Plus, Tesfai knew that traders trade what is valuable, and he assumed the white tents belonged to traders. These days, the Derg offered money, weapons and other desirable goods to anyone willing to turn in fugitives. So, approaching the group for help might elicit not only a refusal to help, but might yield their detention in hopes of a handsome reward from the Derg.

On the other hand, Tesfai knew that nomads were well known for their hospitality, even to foreigners.

Considering the options, Tesfai realized there were only two: Go around the nomads and stay lost, hungry, and thirsty, or approach the white tents and hope for the best.

Motioning to Aster and Tersit, he started toward the white tents. He recalled his mother, back in Addis Ababa, saying her prayers on his behalf.

Mother, Let your God be listening, even if I don't believe in Him.

The tents drew nearer with each footstep.

LANGUAGES AND GESTURES

Just short of the nomadic tent complex, Tesfai and his companions paused. Among nomadic people, it is considered rude to barge into someone else's home—and a group of tents is a home. The three waited outside to be noticed by the residents. It did not take long.

A gaggle of children dashed out of one tent, intent upon a game of tag. Their delighted shrieking stopped when they saw strangers outside the perimeter. They turned, ran, and started calling to others. Tesfai realized he did not understand these nomads' language.

A young man emerged from the nearest tent. He approached Tesfai and the women, proceeding cautiously, appraising them and the desert beyond. He talked softly.

To his amazement, Tesfai heard a response from behind him; it was Aster. She and the young man spoke quietly but animatedly for a few moments. Aster pointing first in the direction they had come, then gestured in the direction they hoped to go. Tesfai could hear the pleading in Aster's voice, speaking what he would learn was a dialect of the Oromo language.

The young man nodded, motioning toward the tents. Aster turned to her companions. "His name is Mohammed," she indicated. "His father is away, but he will return tomorrow. He believes his family might be willing to help us, but they will have to discuss it with the rest of their clan."

Mohammed motioned more emphatically and spoke again. "He wants us to come in. His family will hide us until a decision has been made, but we need to get into a tent before we are noticed by anyone else in the desert. He's a little scared, but I think he feels sympathy for us. The final decision will be up to all the men, once they return."

Tesfai inclined his head gratefully to Mohammed, stretching out his hands in peace. Mohammed offered the merest hint of a smile, and directed another question toward Aster. Aster translated. "He wonders if we are hungry." At this, Tesfai laughed appreciatively, joined by Mohammed. Children's faces sneaked curious peeks from their tents at the newcomers, watching as Tesfai, Tersit, and Aster followed Mohammed into the circle of tents. away from any prying eyes.

Tesfai found himself thinking: Mother, thank you for the prayers. Perhaps they are helping, or maybe I am just lucky.

FEAR AND TRUST

When Mohammed's father Khalid returned to the compound, he heard the stranded travelers' story and agreed that his family should help them. Now Khalid and Mohammed were meeting with the elders of the larger nomadic community. Tersit, Aster, and Tesfai were awaiting the decision. They had learned this clan was part of the Issa people.

The Issa tribe had inhabited this stretch of desert, in eastern Ethiopia alongside present-day Djibouti, for hundreds of years. Herders and traders, they knew the formal and informal routes between Diredawa and Djibouti the way urban people know their way around a small city block. The Issa were also Muslim, close knit, and wary of foreigners. Tesfai and his female companions were nothing if not foreigners and, as Aster had explained earlier to Mohammed, foreigners on the run from the Derg government. As independent as the Issa continued to be, they were not immune from Derg pressure.

Tesfai wondered which would win out in the elders' discussions, their hospitable nature or their distrust of strangers? Tesfai waited, listened, ears straining to hear any of the conversation in the far tent. Even though he did not know their language, he tried to discern by vocal tone which way the decision was going.

Finally, after what seemed a lifetime, Mohammed and his father reappeared. They looked tired, but calm.

"We've gotten permission," announced Khalid. "The elders beg forgiveness for the rude behavior of your guides, Abdullah and Mohammed, for robbing you and then leaving you unattended in the desert. It is not our way to treat people so unkindly, especially after a deal has been struck." Khalid went on. "As members of our tribal group, even though not part of our clan, they have embarrassed us."

Tesfai offered a smile of relief. "We are deeply grateful for your willingness to help us. I do not know how we could ever repay you."

"Payment is not necessary," responded Khalid. "Please, we do this to atone for our tribal members who have harmed you. My son, Mohammed, will take you to the Djibouti border. He knows the way and will accompany you as far as he can. Then he'll show you how to cross the border. It will be a little tricky without your documents, but not impossible. Do you like hiking?"

"We've managed to get this far. Surely we can hike into Djibouti whichever way Mohammed takes us."

"You start tomorrow morning, then," said Khalid. "We only ask that you follow all Mohammed's directions and avoid calling attention to yourselves along the way."

Mohammed spoke up. "You'll be under my protection; that and Allah's. But please do not mention our help to anyone outside our tribe. We don't want to be punished for helping you."

Tesfai gratefully assented. He stood for a long while, his head down, and pondered the kindness of this foreign tribal family with a different religion. They were acting on his behalf, with no advantage to be gained for themselves. Perhaps, he wondered, there is a lesson to be learned from Khalid's and Mohammed's gracious unselfishness.

CROSSING INTO DJIBOUTI

The caravan's pace slowed. For nearly two weeks Tesfai, Aster, and Tersit had been under Mohammed's guidance and protection. First, they traveled just with Mohammed. Then, Mohammed decided they would join other traders also heading to Djibouti. Finally, yet more traders joined them to make a larger assembly, all carrying Ethiopian goods in exchange for merchandise from Djibouti to take back to Ethiopia.

Tesfai leaned over to Mohammed. "I've never seen so many camels in my life!"

The Mohammed smiled at the comment. Then he spoke softly. "We are slowing down. Soon all the traders will be buying and selling at the border. People cannot cross, but merchandise can."

"That leaves us with a problem," sighed Tesfai.

Mohamad answered, still whispering. "Only at the checkpoint. You'll still be able to get into Djibouti, it just can't be at the checkpoint. Too many guards from Ethiopia and Djibouti are around. They might let you through with a bribe, but ..."

"We don't have any money. And don't forget, no passports either!"

Mohammed put his hand to his heart, remembering the experience Tesfai and the women had had in the desert. "Passports are not so important here if you know what to do." His eyes lowered, he nodded casually. "See over there, to the right, there are some low hills. As we go ahead, you will move discreetly to the edge of our caravan, and then make your way to the back. While the front of our group is busy at the border, holding the guards' attention, you will walk toward a trail that goes through those hills. The guards will be too interested in our merchandise to pay attention to anything else. If you walk quickly, you will get into the hills before they notice. You will not be seen once you are in the hills. Keep walking. Soon you will come down a hill into Djibouti. No fence or guards; they are both just here at the official border."

Tesfai nodded. "I don't know how we can ever thank you."

"Just don't get caught getting to the path. My family wishes you well. May God go with you." Tesfai wasn't sure about God, but he would never forget the kindness of the Issa people.

At Mohammed's signal, Tesfai, Aster, and Tersit found their way toward the path. As they started into the scrubby hills, Tesfai turned to wave a final good bye to Mohammed. Mohammed offered a slight wave before melting again into the center of the caravan.

The blazing sun moved behind the three illegal migrants as they walked east, until they came down a final low hill. Ahead they saw a small town of tan mud and brick houses with narrow streets, amid swirling dust. A cluster of white tents sprawled along its outskirts.

"This must be Dikhil," said Tesfai, referring to the town he knew was just over the border from Ethiopia.

Aster sized up the scene. "It is small. And dirty. But it still looks beautiful to me."

"My friend Abdul said the United Nations is here. They have set up tents for refugees from Ethiopia. Those tents must be the UN. We'll head there. I see what looks like an entrance; it even has people waiting in line to get in!"

Tersit seemed overwhelmed. "There must be hundreds already in those tents. I was told I have family members there—how will I find them?"

Aster shrugged. "I don't think we will be lonely."

"We are refugees. We've escaped the Derg and the civil war in Ethiopia. We're lucky to be alive. Now we get to take our chances in a new country." Privately, Tesfai was wondering how the UN could care for so many refugees, especially if they kept coming.

Over the next few weeks, he would find out it was even more of a challenge than he originally thought.

ASTER'S PLAN

One morning Tesfai was visiting Aster, as he often did, in the guards' barracks of the Dikhil refugee camp. When he, Aster, and Tersit entered the U.N. camp several weeks earlier, Tersit quickly found her family members and moved in with them. Tesfai was assigned to one of the communal white tents, sharing living space with fifteen strangers. "You will make fifteen new friends," the camp administrator had stated wryly.

Aster, a pretty girl, had quickly been noticed by a guard named Kamil. He claimed her as his camp mistress and took her to live with him in the barracks. "Desperate times require desperate measures." For a young woman alone, the temptations of adequate food, shelter and protection from unwanted assaults exerted an understandable pull.

Each day dozens of Ethiopian refugees showed up at the Dikhil camp, as Ethiopia's civil war intensified. In addition, Tesfai heard about a drought ravaging the countryside where he had been working. Not only was collective farming not working, it made the effects of the drought worse—as he had feared.

He and Aster were talking one day when Tesfai commented on the camp's conditions. "With so many newcomers each day, you are lucky to be here with your guard in the barracks. Outside, the other guards can pretty much do what they want."

"Don't I know it," replied Aster.

"I believe the UN is trying to feed us and care for us; there are just so many refugees. There is a lot of mistrust between refugees, since the camp assigned us to living groups without a lot of thought to tribal or other traditional loyalties."

"What do you do about the dust?" asked Aster.

"What can I do? I try to keep it out of my food and hope there is enough water to wash my clothes and myself. And speaking of food. It's mainly rice with tomato sauce. I don't know where they are getting the tomatoes, the sauce has no taste."

"Are you saying you visit me for better food?" Aster teased.

"Well, your food is better, thanks to Kamil, but I also appreciate coming to talk." Tesfai grimaced, "Worse than the food and the dust is the monotony, which I think gets on everyone's nerves. Fights break out.

And then there is the heat."

"I was listening to Kamil the other day," said Aster. "He is from Djibouti City. The Djibouti people are annoyed they must provide space for a refugee camp, but they get paid by the UN. So that's okay, more or less. Really, they don't want us in the country at all, and they certainly don't want us to leave this camp. But I did talk Kamil into taking me to Djibouti City. Do you want to come along?"

"How did you manage to get the ride? And why would I be allowed to ride along? Although, I would love to leave here!" Tesfai's plans were not to stay in Dikhil.

"Kamil has family in Djibouti City: his wife and a couple of kids. He's got vacation time to go see them. Tomorrow he will drive to Djibouti."

"And he's agreed to take us and then drop us off? Why would he do that, especially for you? Wouldn't he rather keep his wife in

Djibouti and you here in the camp?" It was not like a guard to be generous toward the refugees, especially the women.

"I am under no illusions. I am not the first woman Kamil has taken, nor will I be the last. I think, after six weeks, which it will be tomorrow, he is getting tired of me."

Tesfai, slightly embarrassed, indicated he understood Aster's plight.

"If I were to stay here while he is gone, who knows what would happen to me in his absence? When he comes back, he will probably feel guilty and beat me because I am not his real wife. I've seen it happen with other guards and their mistresses. And then, who knows, he could decide he is bored with me, just like I am bored with him. It's best to leave. Kamil has agreed to sneak me into his car tomorrow. There's room for one more. Are you coming, or not?"

Tesfai could make only one decision. "I'm coming. Anything is better than feeling buried alive in this camp!"

THE MAN WITH BLACK SHOES

K amil fulfilled his promise: the two refugees from Ethiopia were deposited in Djibouti City. The city, filled with refugees, absorbed them as it had done with those arriving before them. However, jobs were nonexistent and places to sleep indoors were rare. Only emergency funding from the government kept riots from breaking out as the growing number of refugees struggled for survival.

Tesfai awaited the opportunity to move again, this time to another country. He had been living this way for a year when Ezekiel, one of his fellow homeless friends, found him lounging against the wall of one of Djibouti City's many bars catering to the growing numbers of Ethiopians living in the city.

"Tesfai, there's someone looking for you!"

"Who?" Tesfai was wary. Life on the streets had taught him to be cautious about the people with whom he kept company. "Does he look like an official, you know, like someone from the Derg?" Tesfai had heard of Derg officials visiting Djibouti looking for dissidents.

"He said he's one of your uncles, and that he came from Saudi Arabia.

Tesfai and friends in Djibouti

Is your mother's name Mebrat? He kept using that name."

Tesfai's eyes lit up. "I got a letter a while ago from my mother; she said she was talking to Alem about helping me leave here." The best option seemed to be Saudi Arabia. "Perhaps Uncle Alem is here to take me to Saudi Arabia! Where is this man? It's got to be him!" Tesfai jumped up.

"I told him to wait at the al-Azari Café while I tried to find you," said Ezekiel. "I wasn't about to bring him here until I checked with you. Of course, he didn't look too eager to come with me either. He's pretty nicely dressed; I think he realized he would stand out in our environment."

"Ezekiel, I owe you!" Tesfai began to race toward the al-Azari. "Wait, how will I recognize him?" It had been years since he had last seen Uncle Alem.

"Look for polished black shoes. Everyone one else is wearing sandals."

When Tesfai reached the Café, he stood outside and nonchalantly looked in. Then he saw him, the man with the nice black shoes. He pushed past those loitering outside and cautiously approached the black shoes.

"Uncle Alem?"

"Tesfai?" The man stood. "Yes. I am your Uncle Alem. I've been here for a few days, looking for you. Finally, today, I found the right person to ask. Good thing, too, as I was running out of time. I did not want to return to Saudi empty- handed, for your mother would never have forgiven me!" Uncle Alem stood back, looking at Tesfai. Tears appeared at the edges of Uncle Alem's eyes. Presently he spoke: "It has not been easy for you here."

"No," answered Tesfai. Then he said,

"Uncle, I have a favor to ask. May I have something to eat? I am so very hungry!"

"But of course. What would you like? I notice that this Café has a good menu. Cheap, but good food that Ethiopians like."

"Anything would be fine," said Tesfai. "I am no longer picky about what I eat, just so I get to eat something."

Alem ordered for his nephew, then they sat at a table. He eyed Tesfai's disheveled appearance. "Tell me how you have been living."

"I can count on two hands the number of times I have actually slept in a bed this past year. I wrote brave letters to my parents, but the truth is I have been homeless."

"You got yourself from the refugee camp in Dikhil to here …" Uncle Alem prompted, encouraging Tesfai to say more.

"Yes, I had a friend. She had a soldier who liked her and he gave us a ride here in the trunk of his car. Aster, my friend, went her way, and then I found my old friend Abdul in the Ethiopian district. We have our own district here, since there are now so many of us!"

Uncle Alem smiled. "So how does Djibouti City compare with Dikhil's camp?"

"In the camp, we were given food and tent shelter, but neither were good. We had to be careful about the guards. Whenever they had work they wanted done, they just picked us up and made us do it—like cleaning or weeding or digging. No pay, though often we were beaten or humiliated in other ways." Tesfai blanched at the memory.

"There were people in the camp who tried to steal what little anyone else had. But the worst was feeling like we were in prison, even though they kept saying it was for our protection."

Tesfai continued explaining. "Here in Djibouti City, it's a different kind of prison. There are no guards, but there are no jobs for Ethiopians, and there is no organization for food or shelter. The U.N. does not have permission to set up anything here, and the Djibouti government wishes we were gone. Meanwhile, we don't dare return to Ethiopia!"

A waiter arrived with a hot, steaming platter of food. Tesfai eyed the food like a lion would eye an injured gazelle separated from its herd. As the waiter began to set the plate on the table, Tesfai took it and placed the food in front of himself. Uncle Alem made no complaint.

"So how have you been living, with no one to help and no job?" asked Alem. He watched Tesfai eat the spicy chicken stew. In the Ethiopian manner, Tesfai was using only his right hand to manage the bready injera, scooping up the stew. There were no forks.

"Abdul and I found some old wooden boats on the beach, and used these to sleep under at night. I'm not proud that during the day we did what we had to do. We hustled, we begged, and sometimes we stole. The girls became prostitutes. The men dealt drugs. There were some French tourists who felt sorry for us. They often were generous and then we might get a meal, or maybe cigarettes and beer. My parents would be ashamed."

"Your parents have been worrying themselves sick about you," confirmed Uncle Alem. "We were all working as fast as we could, to get you out of here. It was easier with you here than in the camp, but still, it has been a challenge."

"I know," said Tesfai. "I got letters from home every so often. Somehow the letters got to me, even here. But as time went by, I got more and more depressed. I'm not complaining—I mean, you're here and all—I'm just saying how it has been."

"These things take time," replied Uncle Alem. "There are gifts and favors and bribes that have to be offered to the right people before visas will be granted. All that takes time and delicacy."

Tesfai looked up hopefully. "You mean …"

"I have gotten you a Saudi tourist visa. It wasn't easy. As you might guess, lots of people want visas these days. Those so-called guides in the desert made it harder by robbing you of your travel documents. Visas come with strict time limits for use and for staying. Now that I have found you, I can purchase airline tickets. I will get you cleaned up, new clothes, that kind of thing. Then we will leave for Jeddah. They will not let you on the plane looking like you do now!"

"Uncle Alem! How can I ever thank you?"

"Thank your mother. She's the one who has been begging me to help. One more thing. Once we get to Saudi Arabia, you will need to get a job.

This will be tricky, since your tourist visa will run out, and you will be in Saudi Arabia illegally. Supposedly you cannot work there either. But, there is always work to be had, and all you have to do is stay away from the immigration police."

"I've been arrested by the Derg, I've been robbed and lost in the desert, and I've had to live by my wits here. I think I can manage to stay clear of the police in Saudi Arabia."

"It's also time for you to stop worrying your parents so much," Uncle Alem said quietly. "It's time to change your life."

But he could never have imagined what that change would be.

A DISCONCERTING
INVITATION

"What is your religion?" asked Tesfai's new co-worker.

By now, Tesfai was used to these questions. He had been living in Saudi Arabia for several weeks; he had noticed that religious identity affected where you lived, what you ate, how you spent your free time, what kind of job you held, and the conditions of your employment.

Tesfai, lacking proper Saudi work documents, felt fortunate to have found a well-paying, safe job. He was working as assistant warehouse manager for a Singaporean construction firm. Like others of its foreign born, non-Saudi employees, he was housed in a segregated compound twenty-five miles south of Jeddah, home to the country's largest port.

"See, Tesfai, I've never met an Ethiopian. So, what is your religion?" Tesfai's coworker, Khou, was persistent.

Finally Tesfai dashed off a one-word answer: "Christian." You could never tell if this was an honest question, or the inquiry of an undercover agent for the religious establishment. "I consider myself an unattached Christian." (As in, not Muslim or Jewish.)

His family had been members of the Ethiopian Orthodox Church; "Christian" was an available identity, not one that affected his soul. He no longer identified as a Marxist.

Tesfai's offhand remark made Khou, a young, earnest Chinese man around Tesfai's age, exclaim with excitement. "Christian? Another brother in Christ! Please, you must join our Bible study group. What do you say?" Khou eagerly awaited Tesfai's answer.

"Sure, I'll come. Why not? But I don't have a Bible."

"Oh, that's no problem. We'll give you one. It's nearly impossible to find Bibles in Saudi Arabia, unless you're really lucky, or have, shall we say, connections? Come to trailer number five at six tonight. See you then!" And with a wave, Tesfai's new friend hurried off to an engineers' meeting.

Khou left behind, in his wake, a puzzled Tesfai, who had accepted the invitation out of boredom and loneliness. He hadn't anything better to do. Drugs and alcohol, his previous hobbies, were haram—forbidden—in the puritanical Saudi culture. Even living in a foreigners' compound, there were none to be had; the company's contract put restrictions on such substances. Besides, drinking and taking drugs were more fun with friends, and Tesfai didn't have any of those either in this new country. So okay, why not accept the invitation?

But a Bible study? Was he that desperate? Perhaps so. But more than that, Tesfai was curious, not so much about the Bible but about these Christians who had invited him.

He'd been raised in the Orthodox Christian tradition, but his family only occasionally went to church or read the Bible. His mother often prayed; his father prayed on occasion. But in his experience, the Church represented a cultural artifact. Tesfai was dubious about whether God existed.

Tesfai was aware that there were people in Ethiopia who took their Christian faith more seriously. Half of Ethiopians followed

Christianity, which has existed in Ethiopia for almost 2000 years. However, these fervent believers tended to be—in Tesfai's estimation—poor, backward people with superstitious ideas. The Christian God was for those who had no other hope. With his Marxist indoctrination, Tesfai viewed faith in God as a lucky charm for luckless people.

But Khou was clearly different. He was educated. The brothers in the meeting would be engineers, sophisticated, with university degrees. They'd traveled the world. And they claimed to be Christians. Tesfai was curious about how that could be.

It was a wonder he could keep track of the materials and supplies he was supposed to be handling that day in the warehouse as questions swirled about within his mind. Is it possible that God exists? Can you be educated and still believe in God? Is there something to this Bible study business? Is this something I should pay attention to?

At precisely six, Tesfai knocked on the door of trailer number five. He had no idea what to expect as the door opened and Khou greeted him. He entered, hoping for answers.

THE TERROR-FILLED NIGHT

Tesfai lay on his bed, eyes wide open. Following the Bible study, Tesfai had stumbled back to his trailer. He'd managed to maintain his composure through the meeting; he'd sung the Gospel songs; he'd offered a simple prayer, just enough to fit in; he'd accepted the Bible they had given him. He'd read the evening's passage, and listened to the discussion. But the longer he stayed with the Christians, the more agitated he had felt.

Back inside his trailer, Tesfai was alone and terrified. It wasn't the company. The two brothers had warmly accepted him even though they were all Chinese and he was an African. It was the Bible passage that was the problem.

The words of the Bible had unmasked him as a fraud. Not only was he unworthy of the brothers' company, he realized he was condemned by God. As the evening unfolded, it had become clear to Tesfai that there was a God, and that he deserved only the harshest of punishments from this God.

He jumped out of bed. Around and around, back and forth, Tesfai paced his trailer, going over the words of 2 Timothy 3: 2-5. By now, he had them memorized:

People will be lovers of themselves, lovers of money, boastful, proud, abusive, disobedient to their parents, ungrateful, unholy, without love, unforgiving, slanderous, without self-control, brutal, not lovers of the good, treacherous, rash, conceited, lovers of pleasure rather than lovers of God—having a form of godliness but denying its power. Have nothing to do with such people.

The words his Bible study companions had honored as an encouragement toward a godly life, Tesfai recognized, with horror, as an accurate indictment of his life. Burning with shame, Tesfai went over the list, acting as his own prosecutor before a terrifying God:

"Have I loved money? Of course; I spent freely—and it wasn't even my own money that I squandered!" Tesfai blanched at the recollection.

"Disobedient to parents? Over and over, I told my mother and father I was going to study or apply for work when all I did was go drinking. I was disobedient and disrespectful, and I did all this without remorse!" Tesfai recoiled at the memories.

"And my father, and my mother, how often did they try to set me straight? They broke their hearts trying to guide me—they sent me to different schools, to different towns, they talked with me, gave me second chances, all of which I abused. I refused to go to school, I wasted time and money in Germany. And for what? I was only after pleasure. I thought only of myself." The pain of his selfish and ungrateful life rushed over Tesfai.

"And what of all the girls I charmed? I treated them not as human beings, but just as objects of gratification. I am guilty of being abusive!" Tesfai considered more of the words of 2 Timothy.

"Form of religion? I am a phony. I was brought up to be a Christian; my parents tried the best they could to guide me to faith, but I didn't even believe God existed.

"I am a sinner! God, you will destroy me! What am I to do? Oh, God, please help me!" Tesfai dropped to the floor in a wallow of self-disgust.

His eyes happened, just then, to alight on his new Bible.

Tesfai lunged for it, leafing frantically through its pages to locate the accusing passage. Thanks to his lack of familiarity with the Bible, he did not find the condemning words. He found something else.

Khou and Shen had obtained their Bibles through the Billy Graham organization. Within each Bible was a photo of Billy Graham, a brief explanation of sin, and a way to find forgiveness of sin. Instead of the condemning passage, Tesfai found the "Sinner's Prayer."

The prayer was short, to the point, and exactly what Tesfai craved. Reading the words carefully, Tesfai discovered that not only did God see him as a sinner (this was obvious to Tesfai) but that God provided a means toward forgiveness and a new life. Convicted though he was by the Word of God, Tesfai could plead with God for forgiveness, and receive it.

Calming his breathing, allowing himself to sit down, Tesfai folded his hands, bowed his head, and, reading the words, he prayed:

Dear Lord Jesus, I know that I am a sinner, and I ask for Your forgiveness. I believe You died for my sins and rose from the dead. I turn from my sins and invite You to come into my heart and life. I want to trust and follow You as my Lord and Savior. I ask this In Your name. Amen.

Exhausted, spent, but finally comforted, Tesfai made his way to bed. Lying down, he whispered, "Thank you, God." Then he drifted off, peacefully, to sleep.

He would wake up a new man with an unforeseen new future ahead.

A CONFESSION AND
EXPLANATION

The next morning, eager to tell about his experience, he found one of the Chinese Christians. He grabbed the man and hugged him. "I don't know how to tell you this—but, after that Bible study yesterday, I became a Christian!"

The engineer, startled by Tesfai's excitement, almost dropped his clipboard. "But, wait. Yesterday you said you were a Christian! How can you become what you already were?"

"Yes, I mean no, it doesn't make sense. But it's true! When is the next Bible study? I'll explain everything then."

"Not for a couple of days. But I don't want to wait. How about I call a special meeting for tonight? For the sake of our employers, we'll just call it Fellowship Night."

"I'll be there. Thank you. And remember, last night you brought me to Jesus!" Tesfai took off rapidly for his post at the warehouse. He felt like he was walking on air.

That night, Tesfai and his Christian brothers, Khou and Shen, sat in Khou's trailer. As they drank tea and munched Chinese sweets Khou's mother had sent from Singapore, all eyes were fixed on Tesfai.

Tesfai tried to find the words to explain it all. "Ethiopia has always identified as a Christian society. We've had the church for hundreds of years—probably we were one of the first peoples to embrace Christianity. I was baptized, as a baby, in the Ethiopian Orthodox Church.

"My mother and father and all us kids were expected to go to church. For me, it had little meaning. But last night, in the Bible study, we talked about what it all meant for our personal lives; this was something I hadn't experienced. I have to say, even though I sometimes went to church back in Ethiopia, I never got around to believing in God. I don't think I am different from a lot of others, that is, people who have been born into the faith, but never took Christianity or Jesus seriously. I had to leave Ethiopia to know there was a God, and that this God loves me."

"A Christian who didn't believe in God? That's a new one," one of the brothers said. He didn't realize he had said that out loud, until Tesfai responded.

"Well, yes, but you can do that if you feel that your church only asks you to show up once in a while, say some prayers, and just, uh, go through the motions. And that was me: a non-believing Christian.

"Now my parents, pretty much believe; my mother prays—a lot—and my father occasionally reads the Bible at home. But I was a disobedient son and couldn't see the point. Plus, the Ethiopian Orthodox Church was closely tied to our Emperor Haile Selassie. It seemed to me, if you wanted to get anywhere in Ethiopia, you had to show loyalty to the Emperor and to the Church. And I hate to say this—and I could be wrong—my church cared more about supporting the Emperor than about following Jesus. And finally, I've done some bad things in my life."

"This is indeed sad," said Khou in a low voice. "So, what changed for you?"

"Everything!" cried Tesfai, nearly knocking over his tea as he jumped up. "You invited me to Bible study, you took me in and gave me a Bible. Then, last night, through that Bible, God spoke to me, and I became terrified. I fumbled around, looking for guidance, and I found the Sinner's Prayer—the one right here." Tesfai pulled open his Bible and pointed to the prayer. He sat down, bowed his head, and said, "Last night, for the first time, I came to know Jesus as my Savior and Lord! And here I am."

"No, it's not 'Here I am!'" corrected Khou. "It's 'Here we are', because Jesus tells us that whenever two or more are gathered in His name, He is in the midst of us. That's a promise, straight out of your new Bible."

"And you're smart and educated," the words spilled out of Tesfai. "I didn't realize you could be smart and educated and still be followers of Jesus. But you are; this is something I never thought possible!"

"Ah," responded Shen, smiling warmly. "It appears you have a lot to learn. We have a saying: 'A journey of a thousand miles begins with a single step.' Your Christian journey has just commenced, with your acceptance of Jesus as your Lord. Welcome, welcome to the adventure!"

Tesfai no longer needed to feel like a fraud alongside these devout brothers. They accepted him, just as he knew Jesus had. "It is the adventure of a lifetime," he mused. "I wonder where it will take me? What else does God have in store?"

THE LOST COIN

Tesfai arrived at trailer number five for the regular Bible study with Khou and Shen. The three young men had been meeting in one another's trailers for a few months. They'd studied Scripture, shared their life stories, prayed, and sung Gospel songs together. The two Chinese engineers from Singapore had enthusiastically discipled Tesfai in his newfound Christian faith; they welcomed him as their Ethiopian brother in Christ. So well did Tesfai know his two friends that, upon entering Khou's trailer, he immediately knew something had changed.

They sat where they always sat, around the small kitchen table. Shen pressed the usual cup of Chinese herbal tea into Tesfai's hands. "Tesfai, today we learned that our engineering contract is ending. We will be leaving at the end of the month."

Tesfai tried to look happy. He'd known theirs was a temporary job, subject to termination at any time. Now that time had come. "Your families will be pleased to have you back. Their gain shall be my loss— you have no idea how much you have meant to me, and how much I will miss you!"

Shen spoke up. "As we will surely miss you. First, we've never known anyone—anyone—come to the Lord as quickly and deeply as you have. Why, just in these short months you've grown amazingly in your love for Jesus." Shen then tried to be light hearted. "And then, you have introduced us to the wonderful foods of your Ethiopia, so different from our Chinese food. I think I am as fond of injera bread as I am of rice noodles, thanks to you. And your spicy lamb stews, well, what can I say?"

Khou chuckled, but then became serious, as he noticed Tesfai's distress. "You are fearful that when we leave, you will fall back into your old habits?"

This was exactly what Tesfai had been thinking. "I think I can withstand those temptations, praise be to God. But I am not looking forward to being alone; it is true, I fear what could happen if I am lonely enough. I can only say that I will miss you; I will miss our fellowship, our times of sharing and growing together. I cannot deny it."

Shen spoke again. "Tesfai, you have got to be one of the most social guys I have ever known. So, I can see how you'd fear being alone, especially as a new Christian. But let me tell you something. Keep in mind Jesus' parable of the lost coin. Remember the woman in the story? She cleans her house from top to bottom, then from bottom to top. Why? Because she had ten coins but now finds only nine. She does not stop cleaning until she finds that tenth coin. And when she finds it, do you think she will just put it aside carelessly? No. She will guard that coin with her life.

Tesfai, you are the lost coin."

Khou picked up the thread. "God has found you. You were lost, yes— to bad living, to Communism, to disobedience of your parents, to ignoring God, even when your parents were praying for you. But now, you are found!"

"God found you," Shen stated emphatically. "Remember, the coin did not look for the woman, the woman looked for the coin. Just so, you weren't looking for God, God was looking for you. You can depend on Him; God is faithful, and will not let you go!"

Tesfai allowed himself to feel a little hopeful. "I am the lost coin," he murmured. "God has found me, God is faithful; God will not let me go." He looked at his companions slyly. "Next week, you shall come to my trailer for dinner. You can count on an extra spicy lamb wat and injera bread. And no cutlery either: we shall eat the Ethiopian way, using just our hands! It will be a dinner you won't forget."

Kou laughed. "And we will not forget you, assuming you don't kill us first with your extra hot red pepper stew!"

The three spontaneously set about singing "Amazing Grace.". For Tesfai this was his theme song: "I once was lost, but now I am found."

A SURPRISE PROPOSAL

The Asian Christians left, but Tesfai did not remain alone. He continued his work with the construction company from Singapore, and eventually became a member of a clandestine Bible study group; in Saudi Arabia, while one can own a Bible, it is against the law to study the Bible in a group.

Jeddah is one of the major port cities of Islamic Saudi Arabia, but still, it was in Jeddah that he found the spiritual support he needed. He continued to grow in his faith, even in this city, the entryway for Islamic pilgrims making their way to Mecca and Medina. He became close to the city's small group of Christians, one in particular.

"I have something I need to tell you," Tesfai confided to his prayer partner of nearly two years. The two were meeting after Sunday worship for their usual prayer time.

Abeba Gilazgi was startled. What could Tesfai Tesema possibly tell her that she didn't already know? Ever since Tesfai had found—some would say by accident, others would say by the hand of God—his way to the small group of Eritrean Christians living in Jeddah, she and he had been prayer partners, and increasingly, the best of friends. They had kept no secrets from one another, so she was puzzled.

Abeba remembered Tesfai's first foray into her church, named "The Welfare of P" to hide the fact that it was a Christian church. One of the Eritrean members of the church had run across the Ethiopian Tesfai, on one of those rare occasions he'd visited Jeddah. Seeing the New Testament in Tesfai's front shirt pocket, brother Gebrulel—then a stranger—had asked quietly, "Are you Christian?" When Tesfai assented, Gebrulel had invited him to church, even insisting on picking him up from the compound of the construction firm.

Ethiopia and Eritrea are neighbors with overlapping ethnicities but different languages. Although Tesfai's mother was Eritrean and thus spoke Tigrinya, the Eritrean language, Tesfai was more fluent in Amharic, the language of his Ethiopian father.

Tesfai had spent the better part of seven months as a solitary Christian at the compound following Shen's and Khou's departure. He'd read and memorized Scripture, prayed and sang the Gospel songs alone in his room; he was lonely for Christian fellowship.

Tesfai jumped on Gebrulel's invitation. Each Friday, the official day of worship in Saudi Arabia, Gebrulel brought Tesfai to his "Welfare of P" church which met in one of the American oil companies' compounds. Meeting on Friday was a way of disguising its true purpose, coming together in the name of Jesus Christ.

Abeba recalled with amusement Tesfai's initial encounter with the group. Following Welfare of P's multinational worship service, Tesfai spent time being quiet, listening before learning to express himself confidently in Tigrinya. Now he blabbered like a magpie.

Abeba also knew plenty about Tesfai's past. He'd been open about his shortcomings ahead of coming to the Lord. She knew about the loose living; she'd been present when Tesfai spoke of his infatuation and then disillusionment with Communism. Abeba, though, saw more than a bad boy gone straight. She saw a dedicated, caring disciple of Jesus Christ— who had dared to embrace Christianity in, of all places, Saudi Arabia! She, who had lived all her life as a fervent believer, felt nothing but admiration for this man growing in faith.

Abeba waited for Tesfai to reveal what he wanted to tell her. Tesfai, for his part, took a deep breath and leaned forward. He clasped his hands nervously and uttered the last words Abeba expected to hear: "Abeba, I want to marry you. Will you have me? That is what I wanted to tell you: that I love you and want to spend all the rest of my life with you. Will you marry me?"

Abeba paused, reflected, waited. Tesfai stared at her anxiously. Had he said something wrong?

Then she answered quietly. "I also have something to tell you," she began.

Now it was Tesfai's turn to be startled. Had he come too late? As far as he was concerned, Abeba was a wonderful catch—pretty, well-spoken and intelligent, a devout and fervent Christian. Surely he was not the first to notice; had someone else gotten to her before and how come he had not known this? He prepared to be disappointed.

Abeba went on. "For these last few months I have been fasting and praying." She looked at Tesfai. "It was clear to me that God has great things in mind for you; I did not want to get in the way of God's plan for you. So even though I was beginning to fall in love with you, the reason I was fasting and praying was to get rid of the feelings that I had.

I did not want to interfere with the plans God had for you."

Tesfai sat back, relieved. "I did notice you were getting a little thinner," he said. "I thought maybe it had something to do with those American magazines that are floating around." Abeba rolled her eyes.

"Oh yes! We are really big on American culture around here, are we not? Nope, that wasn't it. I had determined that, if God wanted us to be married, then God would have to get you to approach me. Only then would I know it was God's will that I would be your wife, not someone who got in the way of your journey with God. Our meeting was no accident Tesfai. The Lord must have planned it all along."

"And now I have asked ..." mused Tesfai. "It must be God's will! When can we get married? It must be soon, very soon!"

Abeba held up her hand. "I do agree to the marriage, but now we must have an engagement period."

"What? An engagement period? What for?" Tesfai's delight in Abeba's acceptance turned to consternation. What would it take for this woman to marry him quickly?

"We need an engagement period, because marriage is serious and we need to get to know each other before we get married."

"That's for people who don't know each other," protested Tesfai. "Why, we know each other, have known each other for two years. What can you possibly not know about me? There are no surprises!"

"Well, there was one surprise." Abeba smiled at her fiancé. "I did not know you were going to ask me to marry you."

"And now I know why you have gotten thinner. But neither surprise is enough to warrant a long engagement."

As they continued to plan for their upcoming wedding, Tesfai and Abeba understood their lives would change. Just how much, they would find out in good time.

A NARROW ESCAPE

"Uh oh!" Tesfai's friend Tesfaberhan glanced nervously in his mirror as he started to maneuver his Citroen motor-car haphazardly through the market. His passengers, Tesfai and Abeba, quickly discerned the reason for his anxiety.

Tesfaberhan was a legal resident of Saudi Arabia. Though not a citizen (thanks to his Eritrean birth country), his legal residency status allowed him to live where he wished, and more importantly, to drive and move about without fear of Saudi Arabia's frequent, unpredictable immigration raids.

One of those raids was happening now; the immigration police were descending upon Sharah Makorone, the local North African market where the three had gone to purchase supplies for Tesfai's and Abeba's imminent wedding reception.

Now it looked like there would be no wedding, no reception. Neither Abeba nor Tesfai had legal Saudi residency documents. They'd both overstayed their tourist visas. Both had found work— Abeba to support her family in Eritrea, Tesfai to stop being a drain on his family in Ethiopia. Foodstuffs in hand, days from their wedding, they were about to be apprehended by the immigration authorities, and Tesfaberhan along with them for "helping illegal aliens."

The three started praying, while Tesfaberhan drove carefully but quickly through the market, trying to stay ahead of the police, searching frantically for an exit not yet cordoned off. "Heads down! The police are everywhere. I may be able to get us out of here, but please do not make your presence in my car obvious!"

Suddenly, a way opened. Tesfaberhan guided his Citroen through the narrow exit, a nondescript side street so far ignored by the authorities. Slowly, he drove past brightly colored stalls, finally arriving outside the market, away from danger. He wiped his sweaty brow; only then could he breathe.

"You can reappear now." Tesfai and Abeba sat up, happy to see their apartment complex coming into view. "God is good," Abeba commented.

"His love endures forever," added Tesfai, and, catching Abeba's eye, he whispered, "Just like my love will endure for you!"

Then, from the front seat: "Yes, and I deserve extra helpings of that feast you are going to prepare!"

The three friends laughed. There would be a wedding after all, with a boisterous reception—to rejoice after their wedding and to celebrate their narrow escape from the Saudi police.

UNWELCOME VISITORS

E lsa and Abeba were preparing vegetables for the evening's
dinner. Two Ethiopian couples—Elsa and Fitsum, Abeba and
Tesfai—shared a small apartment in Jeddah, rented from a Saudi
landlord. The apartment's two bedrooms opened off a common
living area and kitchen, in the usual Saudi style. It was normal for
two families to share this kind of living space. For a place in the
midst of Jeddah, it was relatively quiet – "relatively", because one
could still hear horns and traffic from the overcrowded streets.

Tesfai was at work at the construction compound. Elsa and
Fitsum had just returned from the neighborhood outdoor market
with tomatoes, onions and red chilis—all the vegetables needed
for the traditional Ethiopian spicy stew the women were going to
prepare.

Normally, Abeba would be away watching the two young daughters of their American Christian friend, Mark, at his home; but
today she had permission to care for them in her apartment. This
was a special day, with a special feast, and she needed to be at
home to cook. Three and five years old, Courtney and Beth were
scrambling around, busily exploring the apartment.

The women's new Saudi friend, Beti, was with them; Beti had recently started to attend Bible study in the couples' home. A few days before, Beti had declared her intention to follow Jesus Christ. Tonight's feast was to be a celebration of her conversion and membership in their Christian fellowship.

Everyone was in a jocular mood, though Abeba did find herself wondering at Beti's outfit: this morning she'd arrived covered from head to toe in the black abaya cloak favored by Saudi clerics as appropriate women's dress. That was not so unusual for a Saudi woman; it was common practice, lest a woman fall afoul of the authorities. What was unusual was her insistence upon wearing it even inside the house.

Suddenly, the front gate's buzzer sounded. Abeba, Fitsum, and Elsa looked at each other, puzzled. Mid-morning was too early for any guests to arrive. The buzzer sounded again, impatiently.

"I'll go see," said Abeba. She went to the front gate and started to open it partway, intending to peer out. To her surprise, instead of politely standing outside and stating their business, an imposing man strode purposely by her, entering the apartment's courtyard. Then another man stepped past her, then a third. The three were wearing traditional white Saudi male clothing, long white robes and head coverings. Yet a fourth man – obviously a policeman – entered, followed by, finally, a woman robed in black.

Abeba started to tremble. Were she and Elsa in danger of being arrested? Their offense: preaching the love of Jesus to a Muslim woman, a crime under both Saudi religious and civil law.

The first man identified himself, needlessly, as a Muslim cleric. "Ladies, we understand you have been practicing the religion of the infidels, and even encouraging our own Saudi people to do so. This is haram— forbidden. But Allah is good, so we are going to now search your apartment to see if we are, perhaps, mistaken."

With that, the clerics set to work, observed by the police-man and the woman. They pulled out drawers and dumped con-tents on the floor. They overturned furniture, opened closets and hauled out clothing. They swept books and papers off the few bookshelves. In the end, the men piled what they consid-ered incriminating evidence in the middle of the living room floor—Bibles, evangelistic tracts, tapes, books, and song collec-tions. All were Christian. All were enticements to know Jesus as Lord. All were potential tools for evangelizing Muslims. All were forbidden.

"I see we have received correct information." He gestured to the pile and swept his gaze across the women, including Beti. This is all we need.

You will all be taken to jail. Now."

Beti appeared composed as she spoke. "Yes, to the jail; we understand."

Abeba sucked in her breath; how could she warn Tesfai? Thinking quickly, she spoke up. "Yes, yes, we know, we must accompany you to the jail. But see here, I am caring for these two small daughters of my American employer." Abeba emphasized the word American, knowing how closely Americans and Saudis worked together in Saudi Arabia's oil production. Saudis, even Saudi religious police, would not want to annoy American business people nor, for that matter, the American government. "So," Abeba continued, "on our way to the jail, we must leave the girls with their father. It is not right for such young children to see the jail, and I do not want their father to worry."

"Agreed," responded one of the clerics. "But we leave now."

Grabbing their cloaks, the women could do nothing but follow the Saudi delegation to the waiting cars. Behind them, their feast would languish, uneaten and uncelebrated.

MARK'S SURPRISE VISIT

"Mark! What are you doing here?" Tesfai looked up from doing his accounts at the construction firm. Mark pulled Tesfai aside. Since Tesfai's office was twenty-five miles from Jeddah, and since Mark's work was in Jeddah, there was no reason for him to be in Tesfai's office this afternoon.

Then Tesfai took a closer look at his friend. Mark's face was pale, his hands shaking. "There's something wrong."

Mark nodded, running his hands anxiously through his hair. "It's Abeba," he responded. "She's been arrested, along with Elsa! They are accused of proselytizing Muslim women. I've come to tell you, and to take you back to Jeddah. How fast can you get away from the office?"

Tesfai's jaw dropped. "What! How do you know they've been arrested?"

"Late this morning, I was working at my home office. Suddenly, two cars of Saudi religious police pulled up. They got out, then they brought out

Abeba, Elsa and my two daughters. It looks like the Saudi authorities had gone to your house on a tip. They ransacked the place looking for Christian materials."

"Of course, they found what they were looking for. But why did they go to your home?"

"Abeba was able to talk the police into delivering my daughters to me before going to jail. She was able to convince them that two young American girls should not see the inside of a Saudi jail." Mark put his arm on Tesfai's shoulder. "Your Abeba is resourceful; when the police brought the girls to me, I learned about her arrest. It was a clever way to get the word to you! No doubt she knew I would travel here to get you!"

Mark and Tesfai, along with other Christians in Saudi Arabia, knew the consequences for reaching out to Muslims with the Gospel of Jesus Christ. At one time, Christians and Muslims lived peacefully together in the Saudi kingdom. Then, starting in the early 1980s, Saudi Arabia became increasingly dominated by fundamentalist Islam. In return for absolute loyalty to the Saudi royal family, stern Muslim clerics were allowed to regulate Saudi society and culture in restrictive and intrusive ways. There were new limits on music, art, and dance; women were treated as property of male relatives; prayer times and holy days were strictly enforced. Muslims were forbidden from exploring other religions, let alone converting. It followed that anyone reaching out to Muslims with the Gospel could expect harsh punishment.

Tesfai spoke his thoughts aloud. "We made our household a gathering place for prayer and Bible study. All of us felt the desire for prayer, for study, and for a place to tell anyone we could about the Good News.

We've had several Muslims come and visit with us."

"Apparently one of your visitors was an informer," said Mark. "I'm taking you back to Jeddah. Let's go!"

Tesfai made a fast call to his supervisor, then the two men hurried to Mark's car. Mark kept the car at the speed limit as the two men continued talking. Traffic along the main road to Jeddah was not yet clogged with rush hour commuters.

Tesfai was feeling the urgency. "I've got to get Abeba and Elsa out of jail! But how? I will go to the Saudi authorities right away, but will they listen to me? I don't have immigrant status here. I could be arrested too."

Mark understood. "You've told us that when you, Abeba, and Elsa came to Saudi Arabia, you let your visas expire. What does that mean, practically?"

"It means we are here illegally and cannot count on any leniency from the government. Only Fitsum has legal documentation to be in Saudi Arabia. In any case, each of us could be arrested for witnessing to Muslims in Saudi Arabia; those of us living here illegally would have additional problems."

Mark nodded, and Tesfai continued. "Remember when we had our wedding reception and Tesfaberhan was telling that funny story about driving out of the market ahead of the immigration police? We were all laughing, but had we been stopped, Abeba and I would have missed our own wedding because we would have been arrested. We've seen it happen to others."

Mark was quiet for a while, staring straight ahead. Then, in a pensive voice, he said, "I think I know how I can help."

"How?" asked Tesfai. He was afraid of being too hopeful.

"Thanks to the leadership of our friend BJ, and the witness you and Abeba shared, I came to accept Jesus as my Lord recently."

Tesfai listened, wondering how Mark's new Christian faith related to Abeba's confinement in a Saudi jail.

"The thing is, I am not just a Christian. I'm an American Christian. As is BJ. We have other American Christians in our Welfare of P congregation. As soon as we get to Jeddah, I will call BJ, and we will get the prayer chain going. Then BJ and I will contact the American Embassy."

"I appreciate that, but we are not Americans!"

"No. But you are Christians, and now you are persecuted Christians. Our President Reagan has been talking about protecting Christians around the world, and I think we can get the American consulate to look at your situation. Plus, the consul general here in Jeddah is a Christian."

"That might work." Tesfai allowed himself a glimmer of hope. "Abeba is a strong woman, that's one of the things I love so much about her.

But living in a Saudi jail, this is more than either of us bargained for."

The buildings of Jeddah came into view. It was time to get busy with Mark's plan.

ABEBA AND THE JAILERS

While Mark and Tesfai were rushing back to Jeddah, discussing how to secure Abeba's and Elsa's freedom, Abeba was in conversation with her jailers.

Two of them, a young earnest man and an older, black-robed woman, entered her jail cell. Rudimentary plastic chairs were dragged in, the jailers sat down, and motioned for Abeba to sit on the cell's floor in front of them. As Abeba faced her accusers, she saw a folder in her interrogator's hands. She assumed it contained information about her. Apparently, she and Tesfai had been known to the authorities for longer than she'd realized, based on the size of the file.

His head was down, looking through the file, when he began to speak: "Mrs. Tesema, you understand our law regarding attempts to make apostates out of good Muslims." 'Apostates' was the term Saudis used for Muslims converting to Christianity.

"Sir, I must answer first and only to God." Abeba declared. "When God asks me to witness to the love of Jesus to anyone, I must do so.

Even if it's to a Muslim! God loves all of us!"

Now the woman broke in. "Mrs. Tesema, you are to be commended for your praying, which you have been doing ever since you entered this prison cell. But you are not facing Mecca! This is disrespectful to Allah!" The woman indicated the direction of Mecca.

Abeba smiled. "God is everywhere. God does not need me to face any certain direction. Besides, if you'll notice, if I face Mecca I must also face the toilet when I pray. To me, that is disrespectful!"

"Mrs. Tesema," the man spoke. "The women guards here have noticed you are pregnant."

"Yes, I am five months along. My friend Elsa is also pregnant. Is it Islamic charity to imprison pregnant women?" Abeba knew the Saudi solicitude toward pregnant women.

"Mrs. Tesema," what is your legal status here in Saudi Arabia?"

Abeba looked at her inquisitors; she was certain they knew the details of her residency as well as she did. Abeba had no legal status in Saudi Arabia, having overstayed her tourist visa two years earlier.

"I have been living in Jeddah for two years, earning money to help support my family in Eritrea. Our country is being persecuted by the Derg government. The Derg is anti-religious; both Christians and Muslims have suffered for their faith. This has been true ever since the Derg took power in 1974." Abeba went on, "I am deeply grateful I was able to come to Saudi Arabia and escape the civil war in my home country. But no, I do not live here officially. Neither my husband nor I are legal residents; we are both refugees from religious and political persecution."

"Why didn't you register your marriage?" asked the man. "I don't have documents here saying you have a husband. You could be convicted of adultery."

"We are Christians. As you know, Saudi Arabia only recognizes Muslim weddings and marriages. We married in a private ceremony. Many people attended from our church, including several American friends." Abeba noted that both her questioners came to attention when she mentioned the Americans. Their backs straightened, and their eyelids blinked rapidly.

The man was silent a moment. "Allah is good and just," he finally said. "Because Allah is merciful, we cannot harm you, even though you have insulted us by sharing your religion with Muslims. But you will not be allowed to stay in Saudi Arabia. I see from your visa information that you entered our country from Sudan. Therefore, we will deport you to Sudan."

"And my husband?" asked Abeba.

"He will also be deported. Our records show he came from Djibouti, so we will deport him to Djibouti," came the answer.

"That will separate us!" cried Abeba, almost losing her composure. "And remember, I am fine months pregnant!"

"We are sorry," replied the woman. "That is something you and your husband should have considered before you decided to preach about your Jesus to our devout Muslim people."

The two stood and the young man spoke. "If you will excuse us, this conversation is now over." They left, taking their chairs with them.

Abeba was left alone. She started praying once again, for herself and for Tesfai.

KNOWING THE RIGHT PEOPLE

Tesfai anxiously waited to hear about his friends' conversation with Mrs. Hammond, the United States consul general based in Jeddah. Abeba and Elsa were still in jail. He had not been allowed to see his wife in nearly a month, since the day she was arrested.

However, ever since Mark's visit to Tesfai's office, the Christians of the Welfare of P church had been meeting and praying on behalf of Abeba and Elsa; no one at the meetings prayed more keenly then Tesfai and Fitsum.

The church's members vowed eagerly, "We can pray, and we can act! We need visas for Tesfai, Abeba and Elsa. Mark and BJ, we will keep calling Mrs. Hammond's office until she agrees to meet with you. Every day, if necessary." Several days later, Mrs. Hammond met with BJ and Mark. Now, Tesfai was eagerly anticipating the outcome of that meeting.

Finally, the front gate's bell sounded. Tesfai interrupted his pacing and praying and raced to open the gate. BJ and Mark piled in, exuberant.

"We've succeeded, praise be to God! Mrs. Hammond will contact the American Embassy in Riyadh to grant you refugee status!" Mark pumped his arm into the air in exultation.

BJ's enthusiasm was tempered. "However, there is still a problem. We explained to Mrs. Hammond about your Christian faith and activities, and she agrees you are being persecuted by the Saudi government because of your religion."

"She was sympathetic," confirmed Mark. "She also reminded us about President Reagan's commitment to Christians around the world. She wants to help with Abeba's and Elsa's release."

"But, the problem?" Tesfai urged.

BJ answered. "The problem is that the U.S. Embassy can only issue refugee visas back into the country from which refugees enter Saudi Arabia. Elsa, Abeba, and Fitsum came from Sudan, so they get refugee visas to Sudan. You entered from Djibouti, so you would get a refugee visa all right, but back to Djibouti."

"Different countries," said Tesfai. His jaw dropped with dismay. "BJ, Mark, isn't there something we can do? I don't want to be separated from Abeba, though if that is the price to get her out of jail I will pay it. But Abeba is my wife, and she is pregnant!" Tesfai couldn't imagine life without Abeba.

Mark reviewed the options. "One is that you and she end up in different countries to start, but then work on obtaining safe passage for you from Djibouti to Sudan and reunite."

Tesfai thought a moment. "I don't think that will work. First, neither government is efficient and, while I was a refugee coming through Djibouti, the truth is, even in Djibouti my legal status was uncertain. I'm sure we would have to clear that up first and that could be impossible."

"There is another way. Mrs. Hammond mentioned that if you were to obtain a tourist visa from here to Sudan instead of a refugee transfer, then you could go to Sudan as a tourist. You'd be with the others, including Abeba. From there all of you would be able to apply for resettlement in the United States, again, under grounds of religious persecution."

BJ frowned. "But we have to figure out how to get you a Sudanese tourist visa."

Tesfai thought a moment. "Debas. From our church. He's Eritrean, but he talked once about having friends in the Sudanese embassy in Riyadh."

"Of course!" exclaimed Mark. "Debas has even been part of the group praying for the women's release. Perhaps the three of us can approach him together?"

"He'll help, I'm sure of it." Tesfai felt hope rising. "We have had other similar situations with the Ethiopian civil war. Plus, my wife is Eritrean."

BJ laughed quietly. "Once again, I am reminded, it's not just what you know, but who you know."

"We need to keep praying. The Saudi authorities say they are willing to deport us, but they are only willing to let Abeba and Elsa out of jail once they are sure we have a plan to leave. That means all paperwork, and we must show them airline tickets proving we will leave."

"That reminds me," said BJ quietly. "The church members have taken a collection. They want to buy your airline tickets once all the documents are arranged."

Tesfai's words caught in his throat, and finally he managed to speak. "Thank you. I will never forget this kindness."

"Remember," said BJ. "My eyes look unto the hills ..."

"From where my help comes," Tesfai added.

"And, we must pray, also from the Sudanese Embassy." Mark's eye twinkled.

AT THE GATE

"Gentlemen, boarding for Saudi Arabian Airlines Flight number 32 to Khartoum will begin shortly. Please have your tickets and travel documents ready. If women are traveling with you, we will need proof they are family members before we can allow them to board. Thank you." The gate agent switched off the intercom.

Tesfai and Fitusm were in the boarding area, along with BJ and Mark; now, they were waiting for their wives. The four men had arrived at the Jeddah Airport two hours earlier, anticipating joyful reunions for Tesfai and Abeba, and Fitsum and Elsa.

Fitsum was fidgeting. "It's almost time to board. Where could they be?"

"Tesfai, tell us again what the Saudi authorities instructed you. Could there have been a misunderstanding?"

"No. They were clear. They told me I had to have all documents in hand to prove we would leave their country. No documents, no wives."

Fitsum had been there too. "Once we had the legal documents, you know, the visas, then they demanded we show them our airline tickets."

Tesfai continued, "We did that, the day before yesterday. We took our airline tickets, for all four of us. They gave final approval, and told us they would meet us here at the airport, at the gate. They would bring our wives in time to catch the plane. It's almost time, and ..."

Mark was nervous. "You're certain of the date and time and flight number?"

Fitsum stood on his toes, straining to see if the women were coming. "Tesfai and I have not seen our wives in a month, not since they were arrested. The police would not let us see or talk to them. We did everything right - we would not make this kind of mistake!"

"The security police were adamant about the procedure we had to follow. Meet at the gate, wait, receive our wives, get on the plane. They even took the tickets to make sure we wouldn't resell them! They want us out."

"Took the tickets?" asked BJ, incredulously.

"They said it was a guarantee. But what if they've changed their minds?" Tesfai's voice faltered.

The four men started down the long hallway toward the airport's gates. Tesfai prayed the whole way, peering into the jostling crowd. "Please, Lord, let me see my wife making her way our direction!"

"Gentlemen, we shall begin boarding. When your row number is called, make your way onto the airplane. Your family members may join you as you board."

Mark and BJ exchanged worried looks. Tesfai and Fitsum began pacing. They looked about to cry. The flowers each had in his hands seemed to wilt in despair, along with the men's emotions.

Fitsum stopped so suddenly Tesfai nearly ran into him. "I think I see them!"

Tesfai looked. "Yes! It's them! I see they have an honor guard. They seem to each have an escort. But they're coming!"

They would have run to their wives, but the police escorts held them back. The small group finally reached them after what seemed like hours of slow motion; Tesfai and Fitsum were so excited they nearly handed their flowers to the police instead of to their wives.

"You're here!" Tesfai threw his arms around his wife. "I thought you might have decided to stay in jail." He wept openly.

"Very funny. We were delayed by a passing royal family motorcade," Abeba explained. "You can believe we were praying the whole way here."

"But quietly," added Elsa, under her breath.

"Gentlemen, thank you for bringing our wives to us. We have been missing them," Fitsum solemnly addressed the police escorts.

"Our job is not yet done," stated the lead official. "We have been commanded to make sure you get on that plane and out of Saudi Arabia.

You may take your Christianity with you."

As the Ethiopians pushed through the crowd, to the gate, Tesfai had a moment to turn toward Mark and BJ. "Thank you from the bottom of my heart," he managed to choke out. "We will never forget this kindness." He squeezed Abeba's hand.

BJ and Mark put their arms around Tesfai, offering him a blessing, and added: "Tesfai, all of this—it was no accident. God has a plan for you. He is going to put you to work! Keep praying and witnessing, and the way will become clear."

ANTICIPATING A NEW ADVENTURE

The runway flashed by as the Saudi plane sped up, then lifted off for the two-hour flight west to Khartoum, Sudan. Tesfai gripped his and Abeba's travel documents, gazing at Abeba in relief.

"I can't believe you're here, that we are here, on this plane." His eyes welled with tears. "How did you manage all that time in the jail? I never stopped worrying. Especially when the authorities refused to let me visit you."

Abeba smiled weakly. "It wasn't easy. Elsa and I trusted in God. Whenever we were allowed to be together, we prayed, and talked about you and Fitsum, and our pregnancies. We never gave up hope that you were working for our release. We had to believe God had a plan."

"How else could we all be on this plane, together, going to Sudan? Originally, they were going to ship me back to Djibouti, and we would have been separated for months, years, maybe longer."

His wife's eyes widened. "Do you think God will use us? Have you thought about what we will do in Sudan? And how will we support ourselves? We're refugees. I'm worried, Tesfai."

"Well, to start with, Fitsum and I do have some money. We sold all our furniture, and the church members were kind enough to take up a collection for us. This money will help with food and housing for a while. But you are right, the bigger question is, 'How will God use us?'"

Abeba had the answer. "There's a big Ethiopian population in Sudan, the jailers told us so. I saw it myself when I was in Sudan before going to Saudi Arabia. There are many who need to hear about the love of Jesus."

Tesfai thought for a moment, "Yes, and Sudan has a large Muslim population, but it tolerates other religions! This is a gift God is giving us, to experience religious freedom. First the Derg government repressed religion for political reasons, then the government in Saudi Arabia wouldn't allow us to practice Christianity openly."

"How will we ever cope with religious freedom?" Abeba grinned at her husband.

"We'll witness to God's love. BJ and Mark told me I have a gift, a calling—not just to be a disciple but to be an active witness, maybe even a minister. They said my life experiences could be used by God. You know, sort of like St. Paul. He wasn't a believer, but then he became a fool for Christ. Abeba, I want to be a fool, like St. Paul!"

Abeba laughed. "I'm glad I married such a fool! Everything happens according to God's plan, even if we don't understand it when it's happening. There is Gospel work we can do in Sudan, I'm sure of it!"

"While we're waiting for our applications to be processed, for entering the United States, we can use this time for God's glory!"

"Speaking of time," Fitsum interrupted from behind Abeba and Tesfai.

"It looks like it is about time to land in Khartoum."

Sure enough, the low-slung buildings of Khartoum appeared in the near distance, in the midst of a vast desert.

"Our next adventure. What God does have in store for us now?" The answer would surprise Tesfai, even though he had become accustomed to God's mysterious ways.

THE BEYENES

Pastor Beyene's wife was adamant. Arms crossed, she spoke firmly to Tesfai and Fitsum. Pastor Beyene sat listening, seeming embarrassed.

"Tesfai, Fitsum, you have been here almost two weeks. My husband and I were happy to offer you and your wives a place in our home. But the friend you brought with you, this has been a big problem."

Tesfai and Fitsum began to object.

"No, let me finish. Pastor heard your story when you arrived at this compound. You were correct in looking for the church as soon as you came to Sudan. You found us, and it is always a blessing to meet other Christians. Of course, everyone here at the Sudan Interior Mission was inspired by all you went through in Saudi Arabia. SIM asked us to offer hospitality to you, and we did. Who could refuse two young Christian couples deported from Saudi Arabia, the women just out of jail, all because of your devotion to God? And we live right on the grounds inside the SIM compound, so yes, we agreed." She nodded to her husband.

"Our house is small," added Pastor Beyene. "But compared to what you experienced in Saudi Arabia it was only a tiny sacrifice for us to share it with you. But your friend ..."

Tesfai spoke. "Actually, she's not so much a friend as a needy person. Elsa and Abeba adopted her in prison. She's Ethiopian, she's Muslim, she was deported with us, she has no family..."

"And she's mentally ill!" exclaimed Mrs. Beyene. "Look, I understand you want to help her. You've all been praying over her, Elsa and Abeba have been caring for her, but yesterday she took all her clothes off and went running outside naked and screaming. I have young children, and I can't have them exposed to this."

Pastor Beyene turned to Tesfai and Fitsum. "Praying is good. Caring is good. But sometimes the best way to care for someone in need is to find appropriate help for them. Your friend needs to be in the hospital. We will take her there."

"Are you saying prayer is not effective?" asked Fitsum.

"I'm saying God has many ways of helping those in need. In this case, when there is a facility that knows how to care for people with mental illness, that is the answer to your prayers."

Mrs. Beyene added, "Be careful that you don't make your friend's illness about you, and about how hard you can pray. Let her get professional help!"

Pastor Beyene looked away, and said in a low voice, "My wife and I are sorry. We must insist you leave our house. We understand you cannot abandon your friend, but having five of you here, and soon two babies— this is impossible."

Mrs. Beyene spoke again, not unkindly. "So here is what we can do. I will take your friend to the hospital. My husband will show you where you can sleep tonight. I'm offering to keep your wives here with our family until you find a safe place where all of you can live. As a woman, I cannot allow two other pregnant women just to live out on the streets!"

Mrs. Beyene concluded, "You may certainly visit your wives, but you yourselves may no longer stay here."

Fitsum and Tesfai exchanged glances, and Tesfai spoke. "We meant no harm, and we regret the unhappiness we caused for your family."

Pastor Beyene spoke up again. "In the short time you've been here, I've seen your zeal for the Gospel. Perhaps there is a place for you to share that with people who need it, people who live out in the city. I believe God has work for you outside this SIM compound. All the people fleeing Ethiopia's civil war are out there. Find them, then tell them about Jesus!"

Something in Tesfai's spirit understood this direction and agreed. Go where the people are. Yes, that is what we should do. But, where will we find an income? How will we eat? Where will we live? How can we survive in this new country?

FINDING THEIR WAY

With Pastor Beyene's assistance, Tesfai and Fitsum found themselves in the Ethiopian section of Khartoum. Though the activity in the streets was vibrant, with its mix of street vendors, outdoor and indoor restaurants and food stalls, and dilapidated storefront shops selling a variety of Ethiopian spices, foods, and household items, an air of uncertainty showed on the faces. The Tigrinya language of Eritreans could be heard alongside the Amharic of the Ethiopians. The refugees had differing political and religious identities and loyalties, but lived and moved among one another.

"People continue to arrive each day from Ethiopia," said Pastor Beyene. "They're fleeing civil war and deteriorating economic conditions. Perhaps you have heard about the Derg's attempts to collectivize everything from agriculture to industry?" Tesfai had been part of that effort; he nodded agreement as the pastor continued. "The people did not appreciate being told what to do by the government. We've all been hearing about blatant corruption and mismanagement of those programs."

Fitsum nodded. "Meanwhile, there was the Red Terror, with the Derg persecuting political enemies, as the leaders became

86

increasingly paranoid about who was an enemy. People have been arrested for no reason, thrown in jail, tortured, killed—some for not being communist enough."

Pastor Beyene filled in more detail. "In addition to the fight between the Derg and the Ethiopian People's Revolutionary Front, there is the Eritrean Liberation Front fighting for Eritrea to be its own country instead of part of Ethiopia."

"I've heard none of the opposition groups are unified. Even the Derg is fighting within itself," said Tesfai. "The country is falling apart."

The pastor wiped a tear. "It all adds up to a lot of misery for the Ethiopian and Eritrean people. Like you did, they are leaving."

"And many have come to Sudan." Fitsum surveyed the crowds milling around him.

"They think it's temporary, which accounts for the lack of infrastructure and organization. But for many, this will be their home for years," said Pastor Beyene.

Tesfai felt energized and overwhelmed. "This is where the people are. This is where we can share the Good News of Jesus. But where to start?"

The pastor had a plan. "Start by finding a place to sleep. Go find a lady named Askalu Keshi. She's a Christian, a member of the Ethiopian Orthodox Church. By day she runs a restaurant, and at night she converts the restaurant into a hostel. The hostel caters to refugees, like yourselves."

"What better way to find the people than to live among them?" grinned Tesfai. His next adventure was about to begin.

MEETING SAM

"You say this Jesus of yours heals?" A young man, in his late twenties approached Tesfai and Fitsum. "Did I hear right? I don't believe it!"

Tesfai and Fitsum had established a routine. Each night they rented floor space at Askalu Keshi's open-air hostel. Each morning they helped stack the two dozen camp beds along the sides of the hostel quarters and helped set up tables for Mrs. Keshi's restaurant. Then the two young men headed into the crowds of Ethiopian refugees, witnessing to the Gospel of Jesus Christ.

This morning they were overheard by the young man, who was loudly skeptical. "How can Jesus help me?" he asked, indignantly. "You must be crazy to say such a thing!"

"Jesus loves you, me, all of us, and saves us from our sins." Tesfai was unyielding. "The Bible tells us He even healed sick people and raised the dead. We have a loving, powerful Savior!"

"All we need do is come to the Lord in prayer and faith. God can do miracles." Fitsum affirmed what Tesfai was telling him.

A small crowd gathered around Tesfai, Fitsum and two other men from Pastor Beyene's church. The four believers were sharing the Gospel, but the crowd was more interested in the young man's questions.

Someone in the crowd began to laugh. "Sam, maybe you should try this. Put these guys and their promises to the test!" Clearly, Sam was well known.

Sam stepped forward. "I've been to doctors here and in Ethiopia. No one can help. But you say your Jesus …"

Tesfai spoke with authority. "Jesus has the power to heal, and to forgive our sins. God sent Jesus to share His great love with us! We are witnesses to Jesus Christ and His Gospel of forgiveness and love and healing!"

"Show them, Sam."

At this, Sam took off his shirt, then lifted his arm to reveal a massive growth. "I dare your Jesus to take this away! I tell you, I've spent months going to doctors and experts, and this thing only grows. What can you or your Jesus do?"

"It's true," said a man in the crowd. "Sam's been around forever, and he's had this thing forever too."

"We can lay hands on you and pray for healing," responded Fitsum.

"We'll call on Jesus, and we will pray for a miracle."

Tesfai agreed. "Jesus tells us that whenever two or three of His disciples are gathered in His name, He's right there with them. And if we ask for anything in His name, God will grant it. Well, four of us Christian brothers are willing to pray over you. Will you accept that?"

Sam moved toward them. The crowd watched, some quietly, others deriding. "Words are cheap—God doesn't care about Sam, or us. You are fools." But the four Christian brothers sat Sam down, laid their hands on him, and prayed: "Father, we call on Your great mercy and love to heal Sam. Let him know Your power and grace, and bring him to faith in You. We ask this in the name of Jesus, Your Son, who offered His life for all of us. Amen."

After the prayer, the crowd drifted off. Sam went on his way, shaking his head. Tesfai, Fitsum, and their Christian brothers stood, then continued along the streets, telling passersby about Jesus' love. The following morning, Sam would still be shaking his head. Only this time it would be with delight.

SAM'S TESTIMONY

"I'm healed!" Sam ran to catch Tesfai and Fitsum. "You healed me!" Sam jumped for joy, grabbing Tesfai's arm, clapping Fitsum on the back.

"Hey, everyone, it worked!"

A crowd formed. Someone yelled, "What happened? Did you find a different doctor?"

"No, these guys, they prayed for me! They said their Jesus could heal me, and now I'm healed!" Sam gestured toward Fitsum and Tesfai. "You're miracle workers!"

"No, no, no! We're not miracle workers; we're followers of Jesus Christ; that's all we are. It's Jesus who cured you, not us! We are only servants of the Lord." Tesfai was having difficulty keeping his emotions in check, given Sam's jubilation.

"Sam, how do we know you're cured?" asked one of the men in the crowd. "It could be a set up." The man looked toward the crowd. "There are all kinds of swindlers around these days."

""I'll show you! Who here remembers seeing the big growth I had under my arm?" Hands went up in the crowd.

91

"You! You! You!" Sam pointed and called to those raising their hands. "Come here! Judge for yourselves!" Sam whipped off his shirt and lifted his arm.

"It's true!" The witnesses gasped. "The growth is gone. It's like he never had it." They turned to stare at Tesfai and Fitsum. "How did you do this?"

"We did nothing," objected Fitsum. "We only asked Jesus to heal Sam. What's important is that we're Christians, believers in Jesus Christ, and that we share the Gospel of God's love for all people."

"It's all in the Bible," Tesfai held up his copy of the New Testament. "We will share about Jesus with anyone who wants to experience new life through the Gospel."

Sam, still shirtless shouted, "Count me in! I'll listen to anything you can tell me about this God. I'm healed!"

"Thanks be to God!" Tesfai and Fitsum were awed by this latest indication of God's presence. With that, they quieted the crowd, and Tesfai prayed, "Jesus, we praise You for the love You have shown to Sam."

Gazing at the boisterous crowd, Sam, and curious bystanders, Tesfai wondered Could God be calling me to active ministry? And he found himself praying: "Lord, where You lead me, I will follow!"

ASKALU KESHI'S REFUSAL

Following another busy day of witnessing to Jesus Christ, Fitsum, Tesfai and a few new disciples began heading back to Askalu Keshi's hostel where they'd been staying for several weeks. The restaurant/lodging was in the Telata neighborhood of Khartoum; they wanted to get back in time to help turn her restaurant into the night's hostel, and to be certain of sleeping spaces that evening. Mrs. Keshi always had a waiting list of eager refugees.

"I can't believe how God is blessing us," remarked Fitsum.

Tesfai nodded. "Every day it seems more and more people are asking for Bibles and tracts about Jesus. It's good that our group includes both Eritreans and Ethiopians. We can speak to both populations and show how Eritreans and Ethiopians can be united in the Gospel."

"Yes, it is all thrilling." Fitsum became suddenly glum. "But I miss Elsa! Our wives are away from us, now with our Christian sister Saba. It was good they could leave the SIM compound. I know they have a safe place to live. But I'm used to evangelizing alongside Elsa, like we did in Saudi Arabia."

"I miss Abeba more than I can say," said Tesfai, barely avoiding tripping over a piece of crumbling sidewalk. "I'm thankful our American friend, Mike, told his mother about Abeba and Elsa needing a place to say. If she had not contacted Saba, I don't know what we would have done. And I'm grateful that Saba made space for them in her small, one-room home.

"I realize there's not enough room for all of us, but still. Abeba and I have been best friends for nearly three years—and after being married for not quite a year, she's been in jail and now we're separated, refugees in a foreign country. I pray that somehow God will find a way for us to be together."

"Elsa worries when we are out witnessing. How about Abeba, how does she feel?"

"I wouldn't say Abeba is worried. When we visit she's always happy with our successes and wants to hear the stories. She keeps track of how many people join our group and celebrates each conversion. The only thing is, she feels left out! Because she's pregnant, she can't move around so much, and just sitting makes her bored. Abeba wants to be an integral part of witnessing to the Gospel."

"Like Elsa," Fitsum reflected.

With this, they neared Mrs. Keshi's restaurant-hostel. This evening, however, Askalu Keshi did not wait for them to enter. As soon as she noticed the group coming up the street, she strode from her establishment to meet them out on the street, several yards from her restaurant.

"I'm sorry. I am unable to rent space to you tonight." She stared down at the sidewalk. "Or any other night."

Fitsum's jaw dropped. "Why, has the rent gone up? Have we failed to help out enough?"

Tesfai noticed the evening residents busily switching around tables and beds while avoiding eye contact with him and his companions. Something must have happened that day to cause Mrs. Keshi to refuse accommodations to his evangelizing group. "What happened?"

"What happened is your evangelism efforts have been too successful. People are starting to leave the Ethiopian Orthodox congregations to join you and listen to you talk about Jesus."

Fitsum interrupted Mrs. Keshi. "And this is a problem? How can hearing about Jesus be a problem?"

"Some of the Orthodox priests are upset. They've heard all the talk about evangelism and miracles, and they don't know what to think."

Tesfai's mind raced to keep up. "We're not trying to get people to stop going to church. We just want to witness to the love of Jesus!"

"I'm sorry. I belong to the Orthodox church. I agree that you're only talking to people about what you believe. That's your business and not mine, except ..."

"Except?" prompted Tesfai.

"I was visited by one of the local church leaders today. He threatened that I would be excommunicated from the church—the church I have attended all my life—if I continue to offer you sleeping space. I cannot risk losing my church. I must ask you to leave."

"I see," said Fitsum, a soft smile on his face. "Tesfai, brothers, it's early enough for us to try other hostels. Mrs. Keshi, thank you for the many nights we did get to stay with you."

"Go with God, and please accept my apologies. I am afraid to tell you, though, that this same priest made the rounds of all the hostels in our Telata neighborhood. I am afraid you will not find a welcome anywhere tonight."

Tesfai faced the group. "So, again we are persecuted for our devotion to Jesus Christ. Who would have predicted persecution would come from other Christians? Maybe we have made mistakes. Maybe we should have tried harder to know the leaders of the churches—done a better job explaining what we have experienced. Ignorance causes calamities; arrogance is its cousin." Offering what he hoped Askalu Keshi would interpret as a smile of sympathy, he turned to leave. "Brothers! It's like the early church! Shall we try out the accommodations in the park?"

Tesfai, Fitsum, and their companions strode purposefully and joyfully toward Khartoum's Ginene Park. They were too excited about sharing the early Christians' experience of persecution to be concerned with Ginene's dangerous reputation upon nightfall.

JESUS ON A WHITE HORSE

The companions settled in a spot where they hoped to stay dry overnight. The park was known for its wet, marshy fields and the brothers supposed that if they chose carefully, they could avoid very damp ground, as well as conflict with homeless men loitering about. As night fell, they passed the time singing Gospel songs and reminding one another of their favorite passages of Scripture.

Tesfai spoke first. "Remember the story about Daniel in the lions' den? How many times have we felt like we were in the lions' den, and yet God has always taken care of us!"

"Yes, and the story of Shadrach, Meshach, and Abednego in King Nebuchadnezzar's fiery furnace." This time it was Fitsum who told the Bible story. "The believers were challenged to renounce God, but they refused, and God saved them. Don't forget, those three in the fiery furnace were also exiles from their home country, just like we are!"

Tesfai nodded. "I don't think I want to equate our struggles to that of the prophets in the lions' den or the fiery furnace, but I am curious how God will care for us in Sudan. We've had to leave the Beyenes; now Askalu Keshi and the other hostel owners have denied us a safe space.

What's next?"

The cool, damp air caused Fitsum to shiver slightly. He let his chin fall onto his chest. Then, he looked up. "I think our loving God, Who brought us safely out of Ethiopia and then to Saudi Arabia, and now to Sudan, will find a home for us."

"Of that I'm certain! I'm just wondering how." With that, Tesfai rolled over and began snoring. Soon Fitsum and the others did the same.

Hours later they were jarred awake by a harsh voice shouting above them. "You there! Wake up! What are you doing in the park, at this hour?"

The brothers stirred. Startled to see two men on horseback, Fitsum sat straight up and asked, "What? Has Jesus returned? On a white horse? I don't remember Jesus riding a white horse in the Gospels."

"No, no," whispered Tesfai. "They're policemen!"

Tesfai pulled a hand through his hair, stood and addressed the officer.

"Good evening, gentlemen. We were unable to get hotel accommodations last night, so we came here. I'm sorry for the trouble."

"Yes, trouble!" responded the first officer. "And now we must arrest you and take you to jail for loitering and for causing a disturbance!"

Fitsum was still waking up, and was not yet coherent. "We must have been snoring very loudly. My wife complains about that often. Will you allow us to snore in jail?"

"What, you are married? Why are you here, then? Problems at home?"

"It's a long story. We can tell it to you on the way to jail. We're witnesses to Jesus Christ! We can tell you about Jesus while we are walking beside you."

The first policeman narrowed his eyes, leaned over his horse, and snorted: "Ah, Christians! Thank you, but we don't want to hear about your Jesus. And we are not taking you to jail. But surely you have money.

That we will take."

Jumping off their mounts, they made the men empty their pockets. Tesfai, Fitsum and the other Christian men were relieved of the small change each was carrying. Then, riding off, the policemen commanded "Do not stay in this park tomorrow night. Or we will take you to jail. Tonight, we shall be merciful. Besides, it's nearly morning." They laughed as they moved off.

Tesfai, Fitsum and the others looked at one another. "I guess they were more interested in money than in Jesus. But they missed the chance to hear about Jesus." Tesfai, momentarily feeling sad at the lost opportunity, suddenly perked up. "This night is over. We were not beaten or killed. I tell you, by tomorrow night we can trust God to find us new shelter!"

"Perhaps one without mosquitoes," came the answer. "Ginene Park accommodations come with mosquitoes."

SABA'S HOUSE GETS MORE CROWDED

Abeba, Elsa, and Saba were finishing their morning coffee when Fitsum and Tesfai arrived. The women took one look at the men and fell silent.

"What happened to you?" demanded Abeba. "You look like someone has been sticking needles into you!"

"Mosquitoes."

"Mosquitoes?" asked Elsa. "What's this about mosquitoes?"

"Has Askalu Keshi started offering accommodations to mosquitoes?" Saba joined the questioning.

Fitsum started the explanation. "We did not sleep at Askalu Keshi's last night. We were at the park."

Abeba dropped the coffee cup she was holding. "The park! What park?

What happened to make you go to the park and sleep overnight?"

Tesfai tried to calm his pregnant wife. "Apparently, our evangelism efforts have been too successful. You know all those tracts we've been handing out?"

"I know you ran out of them," offered Abeba. "But what does that have to do with Askalu Keshi?"

This time Fitsum answered. "The priests of the Ethiopian Church are angry. You remember that the group started with Tesfai and myself, then added others. Saba, you remember how your son Mike joined us. He was always a believer, like you, but he wanted to help us spread the Gospel."

Saba smiled. Her son often talked about the group's witnessing to other Ethiopian refugees.

"Then Sam joined us. Sam, the one Jesus healed after our prayers. And Sam brought his friends. Others heard about us, I mean, they heard about Jesus. We kept getting more people joining our group to hear about Jesus' love."

"How can hearing about Jesus be a problem?" Abeba was puzzled.

"Because many of the new people came to us from the established Ethiopian churches. These were people who felt something was missing. Between the tracts and the Bibles and the witnessing, and that miracle when God healed Sam, the local people were starting to feel like they were loved by God. Word got back to the church leaders. They worry about losing members."

"And?" Elsa was getting impatient.

"A couple of the leaders went to Askalu Keshi, and not just her, but all the hostel owners who are Ethiopian Orthodox and threatened them with excommunication if they continued to give us shelter." Fitsum took Elsa's hand. "When we found this out, last night, it was too late to think about coming here. Anyway, we know how crowded it is here. The others could have gone to their homes, but they wanted to go with us to tell people in the park about Jesus. When it became late, we decided to sleep in Ginene Park."

"Ginene Park! That's a dangerous place at night!" Saba's worry was evident.

"Well, we only had problems with mosquitoes. And the police."

"The police?" Elsa grabbed Fitsum's shoulder.

"I suppose that is their job, and they did threaten to take us to jail for being a public nuisance."

"Instead, they robbed us, and told us not to return!" Tesfai finished the story.

"This is unacceptable! You need a place to stay. A place that is safe. I invite you to stay here, with me!" Saba spoke firmly.

"But your home is crowded. We would be grateful for the hospitality, and I am already thankful for your hospitality to Abeba and Elsa, but are you sure?"

"We are all refugees, and we have had worse conditions to live in, all of us. I cannot allow you to be unsafe, so I insist you come and stay here, even if I just have this one little room right on the street."

"And four children," said Abeba.

"And four children. And soon, we will have two more." Saba looked at Elsa and Abeba. "Two more adults will not make such a big difference. Anyway, you'll be safe from more harassment, either from priests or police."

Tesfai was elated. "You, Saba, are a gift from God! And since you live in a different neighborhood, Amarat, we can tell new people about Jesus!"

"Always thinking, my dear husband, you're always thinking." Abeba smiled.

GETTING THE ROOM AT SIM

Tesfai approached the SIM office. "A word with you?" he asked as he poked his head into the small room.

"Ah, Tesfai!" Steve, one of the SIM missionaries, greeted him. "We keep hearing wonderful things about your witnessing efforts all around Khartoum. It takes an Ethiopian to reach other Ethiopians."

"God has been good to us. We could share the Gospel in our first neighborhood, Telata, when we stayed there with Askalu Keshi. Now we are with our Christian sister, Saba, in Amarat, sharing the Gospel in her neighborhood. Of course, we've been inviting people to come here for Sunday worship."

"Wonderful, wonderful!" replied Steve. "So, about this word you wanted to have?"

"I'm wondering if it's time to give us a real room for our worship. As you know, we've been meeting under a tree during worship hour," said Tesfai.

"I'm aware of that. Pastor Beyene is aware of that. Is there any reason you and your group can't join Pastor Beyene's congregation?

He's a good preacher, and I see your wife already attends services with him. Why not you and your group?

"My wife is Eritrean and completely at home with Eritrea's Tigrinya language," explained Tesfai. "Our Eritrean converts have been attending Pastor Beyene's church. However, several others are Ethiopians and more comfortable with the Amharic language. Until a few weeks ago, SIM actually gave us Ethiopians a space to meet indoors. Not that I don't like our tree, but we're getting a little too big for all of us to fit under its shade!"

"Tesfai, SIM gets a lot of its funding from Canadian believers. The reason you had that space before is because your group was started by Ethiopian pilots—army officers who deserted from the Derg government. They were here, practicing their Christian beliefs, while waiting to be granted refugee status in Canada. Now they're gone to Canada."

"Yes, I understand. The Amharic-speaking pilots went to Canada and our group got a lot smaller, and a lot less wealthy. Only I, Lebamu and Marthe remain," responded Tesfai. "But the three of us have welcomed new members. Samuel, the one for whom we prayed a while back, he's here. And he brought his friends. We've grown. Far larger than when I starting worshiping with the army officers who went to Canada. With the army guys, we were eight. Now we are twenty-five."

"Hmm," said Steve, drumming his fingers on the desk.

"Every day Fitsum and I go out to evangelize, just like the early Christians did. We're able to talk to both Eritreans and Ethiopians, and we give out the tracts and Bibles we get from SIM and the Bible Society. We also give out the ones in Sudanese Arabic. Everyone gets invited to church here at SIM. When people come, there is a place for the Eritreans and Sudanese in Pastor Beyene's church. But Amharic speakers, there's no place for us." Tesfai looked at Steve hopefully. "I think it's a hospitality issue. Just as the first apostles reached out to all languages and peoples, shouldn't we do the same?"

Steve smiled at Tesfai. "Let me talk to the others. You've made a good case. I think we can find you a room by next Sunday. Will that do?"

Tesfai clasped Steve's hand, thanking him profusely. On his way back home to Abeba, Tesfai praised God. "First you find us a home. Now, you find us a meeting place. What next?"

"What next" would present the next challenge, sooner than Tesfai expected.

A SUMMONS

"Tesfai, we'd like to meet with you in our office." Glen, one of the missionaries, caught up with Fitsum and Tesfai as they were preparing to leave the SIM compound with another batch of Christian tracts and Bibles.

Tesfai's Amharic group had been meeting for several weeks in the room assigned by SIM staff. The group had grown. Tesfai had gained confidence and expertise in his preaching and teaching despite having no formal training. Outside Sunday worship services, he and Fitsum continued to be active in several Khartoum neighborhoods: Etnine, where the SIM compound was; Telata, where they'd first stayed with Askalu Keshi; and Amarat, around Saba's home. That morning Saba had suggested that the group move to the Jiref neighborhood. She had found living quarters there that would offer more room.

"A new neighborhood in which we can witness!" Tesfai and Fitsum had been collecting literature to take to Jiref when Glen found them.

"Can the meeting wait?" Fitsum gestured to their packages. "As you can see, we've got our hands full!"

"No. Fitsum, you need not attend; we only need to speak with Tesfai. It's about the Amharic group. Tesfai, come with me." Tesfai and Fitsum exchanged concerned looks. Glen's statement sounded more like a summons than an invitation.

Fitsum reached for Tesfai's package. "Tesfai, leave the literature with me. After the meeting, I'll be waiting for you and then we can continue home together."

Glen strode off and motioned for Tesfai to follow. "I think I know what this is about," whispered Fitsum to Tesfai."

"Me too. Please pray!" Tesfai hastened to join Glen.

CEASE OR LEAVE!

Tesfai was startled to see the array of men seated, and waiting for his arrival in the SIM office. Alongside Steve was Pastor Beyene, then Mr. Dutton, the director of the Sudan Bible Society, which had been supplying literature for distribution around Khartoum. Finally, there were other staffers Tesfai had seen on the mission compound. Glen took a seat beside the others. The office was small, with one long narrow window facing the rest of the compound; the window had a view of the tree where Tesfai had originally met with the Amharic-speaking believers.

Mr. Dutton began. "Tesfai, we've asked you here to discuss last Sunday's worship service."

"We've heard some disturbing rumors," added Steve. "Something about casting out demons. Can you help us understand what happened?"

Tesfai took a deep breath. "We were meeting like any other Sunday: praying, singing, offering testimony and witness to God's presence in our lives. I was in the middle of preaching when one of the new guys, someone who'd just converted to Christianity, suddenly began barking."

The SIM men looked at one another, then again at Tesfai.

"You mean one of the men acted like he was barking," clarified Glen.

"No, he was actually barking. Like a dog! And then he got on his hands and knees and began walking like a dog among the other group members. This would be hard to do; as you know, the floor is rough concrete, our group pretty much fills the room, and the chairs are made of heavy metal. They're hard to move. Other members became frightened, since not only was this new Christian man barking like a dog, he was pushing chairs and people around."

"So. Then what?"

"So naturally this disrupted the service. But we had been studying the Gospels, and we recognized that an evil spirit must have entered this man," Tesfai explained.

"An evil spirit!" Pastor Beyene was incredulous. "I suppose you thought it was the same evil spirit you tried to pray out of your friend in my household a few months back!"

"That I can't say," replied Tesfai, earnestly. "We all agreed that my friend in your house was mentally ill. But this man, he'd been completely normal in all our contacts and meetings. And now he was acting like a dog." Tesfai rushed on with his story. "Then he started having what we saw were convulsions. We gathered around him, prayed over him in the Name of Jesus. And just like that, he calmed down, got up and settled back into his chair and joined the service like nothing had happened.

Whatever entered him left when we invoked the power of Jesus!"

One of the SIM staffers was quick to speak. "I can't believe this. The man must have had an epileptic seizure!"

Tesfai responded with gentle firmness. "How many epileptics act like barking dogs when they have seizures?" The men were silent.

Finally, Steve spoke. "I am happy you feel you helped this man. However, we do not believe this is a case of evil spirits or demons or anything else entering this man. No doubt he just wanted attention! You did not deliver him from an evil spirit, of that we are certain."

Tesfai spoke again. "Are you saying miracles stopped with Jesus? Are you saying Jesus lied when He said His disciples would cast out demons in His Name? Are you saying the Acts of the Apostles did not happen? Are you saying we should not take Scripture seriously? Then what do you say to this man who was delivered? Since Sunday he has joined our evangelism group, going out and speaking about the love of Jesus."

Mr. Dutton spoke with authority. "We are saying that as leaders responsible for SIM activities, we no longer trust you to lead the Amharic worship group—or any group—on SIM grounds. We are not comfortable with your interpretation of Scripture. Your gatherings seem to be too emotional, with all this praying and singing and laying on of hands and whatever else you are doing! People are leaving Pastor Beyene's church to join your group, and we feel this interferes with the good order and leadership at SIM."

Pastor Beyene looked at Tesfai. "Your enthusiasm for the Gospel is amazing, but you seem to have your own ideas about how God acts in the world. Maybe your lack of formal ministry training is leading you astray. Even though you admire the early Christians and the first disciples, we are hundreds of years away from those early times. The world has changed, and so has God's way of acting in the world."

"But we adhere to Scripture; we trust the Gospel accounts!" Tesfai objected. "Surely the Gospels are as relevant now as they were then.

What about the Acts of the Apostles? Are they not relevant?"

"Relevant, yes," said Steve. "But not as a hard-and-set model. We must ask you to cease leadership. In fact, we have asked Brother Adane, an Ethiopian Amharic speaker like yourself, to take over. You are certainly invited to continue attending as a member, but

Brother Adane will be the group's leader. And the preacher," Steve added pointedly. "Your enthusiasm is commendable, but we feel your approach to Scripture is misguided."

"Thank you for stopping by." Glen stood. "We look forward to your continued partnership with us in the Lord's work."

Following Glen, the other men filed out of the office. Tesfai remained behind, dazed. *Is this also like the early Christians? They did not always agree, either! Dear Lord, now what?*

Then, as if brought along by a gentle breeze, or a soothing drink of water, Tesfai remembered the words of an English hymn he'd sung in Jeddah:

> Great pilot of my onward way,
> You will not let me drift;
> I feel the winds of God today;
> Today my sails I lift.

Tesfai left the office to find Fitsum. It was time to go home.

ABEBA REASSURES TESFAI

As soon as Tesfai walked into Saba's home, Abeba knew something was wrong. "Tesfai," she asked. "What is it?" She drew Tesfai into a corner of the small room.

"When Fitsum and I went to SIM to get more Gospel materials, they asked me to attend a meeting. At the meeting, they told me I could no longer lead the Amharic group,"

"The evil spirit deliverance," Abeba guessed.

"Yes, they said only Jesus and His immediate followers delivered people from evil spirits. I was unable to convince them otherwise. It seems wherever I go, there are problems. We had problems with Pastor Beyene; then Fitsum and I caused problems for Askalu Keshi; I got us a room for the Amharic believers, but that's become a problem too."

"My dear husband, stop sulking. You should be thanking God for all the people you have reached! Many of these people are now going on Sunday to worship at SIM. Who says there can't be something organized during the week outside the SIM compound?"

Tesfai brightened. "This is my calling, I'm sure of it! To reach new people for Jesus. But I don't understand how this can be a problem for church leaders. The Orthodox priests, the pastors and missionaries at SIM. Sometimes I wonder if we're reading the same Bible."

Abeba took Tesfai's hand. "Remember the struggles other believers had. Remember how Jesus and His disciples weren't always welcome, and part of that had to do with healing? Remember when Jesus' followers complained about other people acting in Jesus' Name even though they weren't part of Jesus' group? Remember how Peter and Paul argued over how to reach people, and who they should be preaching to? Paul's epistles make it clear that the early churches and their members did not always get along! Should today be any different?"

"Well, yes, so now what?" mused Tesfai.

Abeba was firm. "Stay true to the Gospel of Jesus. Continue to offer God's healing, love, and hope to all you meet. We live in difficult times, with the civil war back home, refugees here and poverty everywhere. People need healing, they need hope, and Jesus is hope! Keep sharing the Gospel!"

Tesfai's dark mood began to lift. "Not only are you my wife, you are my best friend. And far wiser than I; you see the bigger picture."

Abeba started to laugh, but then suddenly, she blanched. "Uh oh, I think I am about to have this baby! That's the only picture you need to concentrate on right now!"

Pictures

Tesfai's mother and father

Tesfai as a young child
with his father

House church worship in Sudan

Abeba with Abel
in Sudan

Tesfai today

114

A HAPPY ROUTINE

I t was now 1982. Following their son Abel's birth, Abeba and Tesfai settled into a routine. Along with Elsa, Fitsum, and their baby, plus Saba and her four children, they were now living in the house Saba had found in Khartoum's Jiref neighborhood. The new house was still only one room, but it boasted a small courtyard, partitioned from the street by a wall and gate. Tesfai and Fitsum would sleep outside in the courtyard, allowing the women and children to sleep inside.

Tesfai didn't mind. "The good news is that we never oversleep. If the sun's light doesn't wake us, its heat will."

"Just in time for breakfast and morning Bible study." Fitsum looked forward to their daily Bible study meetings.

"We're living like the early Christians! Here, we share everything: food, living space, prayer, Bible study."

"And hunger!" Abeba had overheard them from inside the house. She listened to the men talking as they arranged chairs in preparation for the Bible study. There were no longer enough chairs for the twenty or more who showed up each morning.

Tesfai agreed. "In Saudi Arabia, we never went hungry; we had jobs and money. We had our own place. Well, our own place shared with you and Elsa. But there we weren't allowed to share our faith. Here, we're living on top of one another; we never quite know where our next meal is coming from, but we are joyfully sharing the Gospel!"

Fitsum looked ahead for them all. "Don't forget: there is the promise of leaving here to go to the United States. Elsa's and my applications have just been approved. Yours will be, too, I'm sure!"

"We'll miss you!" said Tesfai. "But in your absence, I shall carry on the work." Tesfai sighed. "We have a happy life. We sleep, eat a little breakfast, have Bible study, have lunch, then go out and witness for Jesus until evening. Then we come home, eat a little supper together and enjoy our families. Yes, we're hungry, but the Lord is sustaining us. I can't believe how good God has been to us! When Abeba and I get to the United States, what challenge does God have waiting?"

Abeba had continued listening quietly while Tesfai and Fitsum carried on with their rhapsodizing, sharing their enthusiasm for evangelizing and their plans. "Tesfai," she finally interrupted. "We need to talk."

ABEBA SPEAKS OUT

Tesfai and Abeba walked along the streets of Jiref. Abeba held four month-old Abel, who alternated between sleeping and looking curiously at the people who jostled his parents. Tesfai had agreed to Abeba's request to return home early from evangelizing, eat an early supper, and take a walk together outside Saba's small compound.

"Something is bothering you," said Tesfai. "Is it something I've done?"

"No, not exactly anything you've done, but yes, something is bothering me. I'm feeling useless!" Abeba was close to tears. She shifted Abel's weight as she carried him.

"How can you feel useless? You care for Abel, you clean house, you make meals, you're always welcoming our Bible study participants, you help with Saba's children, you encourage me. Oh no, my dear, you are not useless. I couldn't do any of my evangelizing without all the support you give me!" Tesfai put his arm around Abeba and drew her close to himself. "Why, marrying you is the best thing that's ever happened to me!"

"Okay, maybe not useless," clarified Abeba. "But certainly left out."

Tesfai face showed he didn't understand.

"It's: 'Tesfai goes out to witness. Tesfai leads Bible study. Tesfai hands out tracts and Bibles. Tesfai preaches. Tesfai gets invited to train other disciples how to witness. Please understand, I am not asking for recognition, and I don't believe I am jealous of all the attention you're getting. That's not the point!" Abeba's words came tumbling out.

Tesfai started to understand. "You're thinking of when we met. Things were different."

Abeba continued. "When we met, both of us were working. I was an independent woman, helping support my family in Eritrea. We each found the Welfare of P church on our own. In Jeddah we did ministry together. Together we encouraged other Christians. Together we led Bible studies and prayer meetings. Together we visited the sick. The only thing we didn't do together was when I was arrested. For witnessing to the Gospel, I might add! I was in jail alone, even though I knew you were trying to get me out."

Tesfai kept his eyes fixed on Abeba. "I also remember our first convert here in Sudan. It was you doing the evangelizing. While we were living with Pastor Beyene, his wife's relative Debesai came to join the family. You befriended him and talked to him about Jesus, and he came to the Lord! Then he joined our group of witnesses in Askelu Keshi's neighborhood. What a gift you were to him, and what a gift he has been to us!" Tesfai smiled.

"Tesfai," Abeba interrupted. "I'm worried about our marriage. And about Abel. I'm not worried about being hungry, though I'm sure Abel would appreciate more to eat. He doesn't understand hunger the way we do, as a sacrifice for the Lord. I'm worried that your work for the Gospel is taking you away from us—me, your son."

Tesfai stammered. "You think our marriage is in trouble?"

"Not yet," replied Abeba. "After all, we're still talking; that is good. I think we've fallen into a bad pattern. You do all the Gospel work, and I do all the housework and childcare. As much as I love God and trust in Jesus, I can't see being happy if this continues."

"We were a team."

"We were a team," agreed Abeba. "Now we are not; at least, we're not a team of equal players. I need to be a part of things, not just the person hidden in the background. I need to be involved in the Gospel work. Surely God can use me for more than cleaning and cooking and childcare."

"A team," confirmed Tesfai. "We will be a team again. Abeba, my wife and wisest friend, God brought us together for a reason, and together we will serve the Lord!" Tesfai pumped his arm in the air.

"Together," sighed Abeba wistfully.

"As a sign that I can again become a real team player, let me carry Abel.

He's got to be getting heavy!"

"I accept your offer." Abeba smiled as she handed Abel to Tesfai. "We can go home now. By the way, I think I have found us another place to stay, one where we can have more privacy and space."

"Another home we will go to, together." Tesfai looked admiringly at his wife. "So, tell me about this new place."

NEWS AND MOVES

"I have news!"
"We have news!"
"Guess what?"

The friends were finished eating supper in Saba's home. Tesfai, Abeba, Elsa, and Fitsum all started speaking at once, then laughed at the cacophony they'd created.

"One at a time!" Saba laughed. "Fitsum and Elsa, you first."

Elsa jumped with excitement. "Our permits have been processed! We will be leaving shortly for the United States! We've been accepted as refugees."

Fitsum filled in the details. "They've found sponsors for us. Saba, thank you for letting us stay with you these last eight months. Finally, we and our baby will leave, and you will have three fewer people living here. I can't believe it! We've been in Khartoum nearly a year, but the time has just flown!"

"Congratulations!" Tesfai was heartily enthusiastic for his friends.

"Hopefully we'll not be too far behind you."

Saba looked at Abeba. "What is your news?"

"We shall be a little delayed leaving Sudan. My younger brother Efrem has been approved for refugee status here in Sudan. He will be arriving soon."

"And he will be living with us." Tesfai was pleased to announce this blessing. "We will be a family of four, with our son Abel and soon with Efrem."

"So we lose three, but gain another resident," commented Saba.

"Well, that's our other bit of news. Saba, you have been hospitable, and we thank you for allowing us to live with you."

Abeba continued, "Tesfai and I have been invited to stay with one of the families I got to know when I was out shopping for injera bread a few weeks back. We believe it's time for you to recover your own space."

Tesfai added, "We were almost through the refugee transfer process to the United States, but since Abeba's brother is joining us, we will have to wait while his application is being processed. We know you need to have your home to yourself again."

Saba smiled. "It has been crowded, but I have enjoyed having you with me. It helped all of us, sharing space, expenses, and food."

"It is pretty amazing how God brought us together when we arrived in Sudan," agreed Abeba. "Now God has offered all of us, I believe, more opportunities to serve Him and reach out to more people!"

"Starting with new friends! But also keeping the old. Abeba and I will always remember and hold each of you in our hearts."

NOT ONE, BUT TWO
BIRTHDAYS!

Tesfai and Abeba, along with their new landlords, Emuna and Tekeste, surveyed the courtyard. All was ready for a grand birthday party.

"I don't know how to thank you," said Abeba, fervently. "We could never have had this first year birthday party for Abel without your help!"

"You've housed us, you've fed us, and now you're putting on this party for our son. You have been a blessing to us in every way," added Tesfai.

"Don't forget how, first, you helped our daughter, "It is we who are grateful." Tekeste became tearful.

"Remember when we met?" Emuna would never forget. "I had my daughter in my arms; she was not well, and Abeba, you offered to visit us and pray for her. You and your friend Elsa came. My daughter improved, and you told me more about Jesus."

"Now we are both believers!" exclaimed Tekeste. "Your brother and sister in Christ!"

Tesfai remembered. "Then, after you came to the Lord, you invited my family and me to live with you! We've been here for almost four months, and you've always made us feel welcome! I know we will visit often, even though we have just now found our own place to live."

"We will miss you and hope to see you often. But listen, the guests are coming!" Emuna inclined her head toward the front gate. The cheerful sounds from the arriving crowd could be heard.

Abel was having a birthday in the Ethiopian and Eritrean tradition, with lots of guests and plenty of food and celebration. The first birthday of an Ethiopian child is particularly important. Tekeste and Emuna were making this one extra special.

The guests began milling around, talking and laughing, when Sofia, one of the attendees, came to see Abeba and Tesfai. She took Abeba's hand, offering congratulations for Abel's successful completion of his first year of life.

"Abeba, Tesfai, I have friends in the town of Gedarif who would like to make your acquaintance. They are Christians from Ethiopia. They've just arrived in Sudan, and they are looking to form a church community in Gedarif. When I was last in Gedarif, I told them you could help." Sofia looked at Tesfai. "Would you be willing? I think God can use you there!"

"Tell us about these friends," said Tesfai.

"Their names are Tesfa, Malaku, and Berhanu. They are part of the Lutheran church in Ethiopia, but they had to leave, like you, thanks to government persecution. They're working for a Swedish charity helping refugees and immigrants in Sudan but they are also looking for a church community. I mentioned how the both of you have been involved with growing the community of believers in Khartoum, and they wonder if you might help them."

Tesfai looked at Abeba. "I am honored. But our problem is that we are about to move into our new home in Jiref Sheta. We've been living off the hospitality of Emuna and Tekeste. The money we brought from Saudi Arabia is long gone. We are unable to afford the trip to Gedarif, much as we would want to help."

Abeba had a thought. "There is a way. I think this is an invitation from God, through Sofia and her friends in Gedarif." She turned to Tesfai. "I will sell my wedding ring. The money we get for the ring will pay for your trip, and then we will see what happens after that."

Sofia looked at Abeba. "Your wedding ring?"

"My wedding ring! I think spreading the word of God around Sudan is more important than hanging on to my wedding ring. Tesfai has already lost his, probably due to all the weight we have been losing. I might as well give mine to a righteous cause!"

Abeba looked at her husband. "Tesfai, Sofia is giving you another means to grow the church. We have been active in much of Khartoum. I believe this is God's will, to have you go elsewhere in Sudan and find more disciples of Jesus. Sofia, thank you for the offer!"

"And what will you do while I am traveling? We are a team!"

"I will stay here, in our house. I will continue with the prayer and Bible study groups, and you will promise not to be gone more than a couple of days at a team! You will keep remembering we are a team."

"Agreed, my dear wife." Tesfai grinned at Abeba, already thinking ahead to the work in Gedarif. "I will ask our Christian brother Debretsion to come with me."

Sofia smiled. "I told my friends they could probably count on your help. Let me know when you are about to start your trip, and I will give you a letter of introduction."

Suddenly, a whirlwind of energy crashed into the three adults. It was Abel, followed by a laughing and out-of-breath Emuna. "Have you forgotten it's Abel's birthday? It's time to start eating!"

"Abel's first birthday, the catalyst for the birthday of a new church in Gedarif," said Tesfai. "Abel is an auspicious son. And Abeba, every day I realize what a gift from God you are!"

A MEAL AND A PRAYER

Abeba and Tesfai sat down to the first meal in their new home in Jiref Sheta. Before they ate, they stopped to reflect on how the Lord was leading them. They felt they had much to pray about.

Though they didn't have a lot to move, it had been an adventure transferring their few possessions from the home of Tekeste and Emuna to their own home. Tired but grateful, they looked at their tiny room, and out the door to the courtyard. Though small, it seemed gigantic since it was just them living in it. Tesfai and Abeba sat close together, Abel asleep beside them.

"Abeba, will you start tonight's prayers?" Tesfai took her hands in his.

"Dear Heavenly Father, thank You for bringing us safely to this new place. Thank You for providing us with this food, and for the friends who have helped us along the way. We want to lift up especially Tekeste and Emuna, since they were so gracious to host us these last few months."

Tesfai continued the prayer. "Thank You, God, for this home. We ask Your blessing upon it as we seek to share Your Gospel with all our new neighbors. Thank You for Tekeste, Emuna, and for all the brothers and sisters in Jeddah who have sustained us with prayers, letters, and even money to help us eat and rent this house. We are grateful for their partnership in this Gospel work!"

Abeba took up the prayer. "Father, You have brought us from Ethiopia and Eritrea to Saudi Arabia and then here to Sudan. Everywhere we have faced challenges—where to live, what to eat, how to share the Gospel—but You have always provided. We praise and thank You for Your care. As refugees and immigrants, we have not always been welcome, but You have always found a way for us!"

Tesfai prayed, "We thank You for all the people we've been able to reach, and we are humbled that You have taken workers like us with no training, just a deep love for Your Son, and made us into Your missionaries!"

"Though we are poor, we thank You for the joy we have in serving You," said Abeba. "We gladly endure hunger and poverty for Your sake. I only ask that You help me find enough food for Abel!"

Tesfai had one more request. "Dear God, keep us safe and our marriage strong. We are united in wanting to reach out to all the Ethiopian and Eritrean refugees fleeing the conflicts in our home countries. Help us discern how best to bring Your message of love and hope and healing to all who struggle with discouragement and fear.

"For all these things, we pray in the name of Jesus. Amen."

They each began to tear off a piece of the injera bread that had awaited them, using it to scoop up a bit of spicy lentil stew.

"Another long prayer, another meal gone cool."

Tesfai laughed. "But our hearts are warm! One day we will remember this time as one of the happiest in our lives!"

"Someday we will have many stories to tell Abel. Now let's eat before cool becomes cold!"

A DREAM, A VISION, A RUMOR

Abeba sat bolt upright in bed. Her pulse raced, she was sweaty—and not because of Khartoum's heat. Though warm by day, Khartoum's desert location caused the city to cool considerably by night.

Abeba scanned the room. Tesfai was snoring beside her, Abel was sleeping on his little mattress next to their bed, and her much younger brother Efrem was asleep in another corner.

She recalled the dream as she tried to calm down. In the dream, someone was knocking on the front gate. It was the middle of the night when no one would be expected out on the streets. Like many poorer neighborhoods in Khartoum, Jiref Sheta lacked lighting for its streets and alleyways. The darkness belonged to thieves and others up to no good—including assassins.

In her dream, Tesfai had awakened to answer the door. "Who would be visiting at night? It must be someone needing help." Tesfai had gone to the door, expecting to find a friend or a church member in need. But at the door was no friend, no church member. It was two or three men who demanded "Tesfai Tesema?!" The men in Abeba's dream beat him in the head and body. Tesfai fell unconscious, and the men fled.

A dream? Or a vision? Abeba wasn't certain.

By this time, several months after their move, Tesfai and Abeba had become increasingly involved in organized evangelizing efforts throughout Sudan. Abeba usually stayed at their small house in Khartoum with Abel and Efrem. She used the house as a base for prayer and Bible study. Meanwhile, Tesfai traveled to the Sudanese border towns of Gedarif, Kasala, and Port Sudan, preaching and organizing church groups. They lost track of how many people were coming to the Lord, but guessed it was in the thousands. It seemed God was using "the Ethiopian diaspora" to promote the Gospel to Sudanese, Ethiopians, and Eritreans.

Earlier in the week, she and Tesfai had had a disturbing conversation. "I don't want you to worry," Tesfai told her, "but on this last visit to Gedarif I heard rumors."

Abeba went still. Tesfai wasn't the type to repeat rumors.

"I was told that our Gospel work has come to the attention of the Sudanese government and the Eritrean People's Liberation Front.

They're both unhappy with us."

Abeba tried to stay calm. "I know Sudan has a large Muslim population, but that's never been a problem before. And Eritrea? The EPLF does not believe in religion at all!"

It's more complicated than that. The Sudanese government is tolerant of Christians, even though Muslims are becoming more fundamentalist." Tesfai took a sip of his coffee. "The problem is that our missionary efforts have been too successful; too many Eritreans are becoming Christians."

"Why is this a problem?" Abeba was perplexed.

"The Eritrean People's Liberation Front thrives on recruiting Eritrean refugees living in Sudan. Sudan's government supports the EPLF because the EPLF is fighting for Eritrea's independence from Ethiopia. Fighting the EPLF makes Ethiopia weaker which is what Sudan wants. So, when we come along and preach the Gospel, Eritrean refugees become Christians and join the church instead of the EPLF."

"And don't fight?" Abeba was beginning to understand.

"And don't fight. "The EPLF is losing recruits for its military, Sudan's government is losing influence in Ethiopia, and both blame the Christian missionaries."

"This is the rumor?"

"No, this is not the rumor. This is what's happening, thanks to the Gospel." Tesfai continued quietly. "The rumor is what might happen to me."

A RUMOR CONFIRMED

"What might happen to you?" Abeba felt her face lose color. "When I was last in Gedarif, I was told ELPF operatives in Sudan want to kill me. Or at least hurt me so badly that I would be unable to evangelize ever again. They are suspicious not just because I am a Christian but because they think I might be a pawn of the Ethiopian government."

"You're kidding! The same government that arrested you and killed your brother Yosef?"

"Yeah, that doesn't make much sense. But the part about hurting or killing me—or us—that's reliable. I heard it from a good source. In fact, I heard it through Tekeste's family."

"Tekeste's family?" Abeba started. "How did they get involved? He and Emuna are our dear friends!"

"It's a little complicated—Tekeste's father lives in Gedarif. When I was in Gedarif with our Christian brother Debretsion, we ran into a guy named Yisak. Yisak is related to the third wife of Tekeste's father. Another thing: Yisak is also cousin to our Christian sister Hereyti from Saudi Arabia."

"Hereyti just visited us a few months ago," said Abeba. "She's one of the Christians who helps keep us from starving here in Sudan!"

"The very one. So Yisak heard about us helping Tekeste's and Emuna's daughter—remember, they're sort of relatives. And he knew about us already from Hereyti."

"What does this have to do with the threat on your life?" asked Abeba.

"Yisak was a fighter for the Eritrean Liberation Front—before it broke up under pressure from the EPLF. Now he's interested in the Gospel, but he also knows people in the EPLF; that's where he learned about the plan to harm me. Apparently, he was able to get the EPLF operatives to leave me alone, at least in Gedarif. It was Yisak who warned Tekeste and me about the threat."

Tesfai thought a moment. "It seems no matter where we go, someone gets upset. The Saudis, the folks at SIM, now the EPLF and their backers in the Sudanese government." Tesfai wasn't sure whether to be alarmed or gratified at the prospect of suffering anew for the sake of the Gospel.

He fell silent.

Finally, Abeba found her voice. "Tesfai, I can handle the moves. The poverty. The hunger. Even the times we've been separated. But threats to your life, that's a different matter. Even the early Christians tried to stay out of harm's way. Tesfai, you must do the same!"

Remembering their conversation and Tesfai's assurances regarding his safety, Abeba finally began to relax. She was about to drift off to sleep when suddenly, there was an insistent knock at the door. It was still the middle of the night. Just as it had been in her dream.

A KNOCK AND A PROMPT

Tesfai woke up, hearing the knocking at the door. "I'll go answer it. It must be one of the believers needing help."

"No! You can't!" Abeba now knew the dream had been a warning.

Tesfai objected. "Why not? We've always been hospitable before. Why not now? People need help, we help!"

"This time, it's not like that. Tesfai, it's the middle of the night. And I've just had a dream about this very thing. It's someone wanting to hurt you.

I'm sure of it!"

Tesfai was startled.

"Listen!" Abeba whispered with uncharacteristic urgency. "Normally when people come calling, they call out their names, even why they're knocking. Especially if we are not expecting them. Listen carefully, Tesfai. Do you hear anyone? Anyone saying anything at all?"

Tesfai listened, his ears straining to hear anything in the dark night's stillness. "No."

Abeba and Tesfai stared at one another. "You say you had a dream?"

"A dream or a vision. Either way, you must not go to that door!"

Tesfai thought for several moments. "Tomorrow I will go again to the American embassy in Khartoum. I'll check on our applications to live in the United States. Perhaps it's time to move on. We've now been in Sudan almost two years."

"You've been able to do a lot for the Christian community here," said Abeba.

"We both have. We've trained leaders of discipleship teams; we've made many friends."

Abeba smiled weakly. "Perhaps our work here is nearing its end?"

"All the new churches we've helped plant are doing well, and they each have good people able to lead. So we are not so needed anymore," reflected Tesfai.

"Perhaps the American embassy will expedite our leaving here if they know you're facing death threats." Abeba looked at her husband.

"Tomorrow I'll check. They need to give permission for us to leave and to find sponsors for us in the States."

"I wonder what life will be like in America."

"When I was a kid, all I thought about was going to the United States and being part of the drug and music scene. Now I want to go so I can serve the Lord. Who would have guessed at the change God has made?"

Abeba was grateful for God's power in her husband's conversion. "I'm certain God will find plenty for us to do. Just like in Saudi Arabia and here in Sudan. I hear they have enough food to eat in America. And lots of Christians, unlike here."

"It will be a different kind of ministry adventure." Tesfai was sure of that.

And so the couple lay back down and fell asleep. The knocking at the door had ceased.

THE JOLLY IMMIGRATION
OFFICER

"Good afternoon. May I see your documents, please?"
Tesfai handed over to the immigration officer the forms he'd been clutching throughout the long trip from Khartoum to New York. After the American Embassy in Khartoum recognized their claim of religious persecution, the family was allowed to immigrate into the U.S. Their route had been from Sudan to Athens for a stopover, then on to New York's JFK airport.

At JFK they'd joined the long line of refugees shuffling toward the checkpoint. Tesfai noticed the photograph of the United States' President, Ronald Reagan, on the wall beside a sign that read March 27, 1984.

It seemed unreal that he, Abeba, Abel, and Efrem were standing before the immigration desk in America.

"Let's see now." The officer looked through the documents, the temporary passports, the visas, the photographs. He peered over the high desk counter at the foursome. Okay, which one of you is a Tesfai Tesema." Tesfai nodded. "Abeba Gilazgi?" Abeba caught her name, mangled by the officer's unfamiliarity with Eritrean names.

"You must be little Abel," the officer continued, smiling at the toddler with big eyes staring at him from his safe perch in Tesfai's arms. "And Efrem Gilazgi, you are Abeba's brother." Tesfai nodded for everyone, as he was the one most skilled at English.

"You are here as religious refugees, I see. Originally from Ethiopia. What religion are you?" the officer asked curiously.

"We are Christians," responded Tesfai.

"Christians!" The man's eyebrows darted upwards. "I didn't know they had Christians in your neck of the woods." Tesfai had no idea what neck of the woods meant, but he did register the officer's surprise at learning that he and his family were Christians.

"Actually, Christians have lived in Ethiopia for over a thousand years." Tesfai felt the need to explain. "As for us, we are missionaries. Missionaries for Jesus."

"Well, you'll probably have to find another kind of job here." The officer grinned. "We've got Christians everywhere in the United States. No need for missionaries, here!"

Tesfai smiled. Someday this encounter would make a funny story, he was sure of it.

The officer went on. "Ethiopians. Yes, you look like Ethiopians. You're all so skinny. I didn't know the Ethiopian famine was also in Sudan.

Don't worry. Here in America you will gain weight, I promise!"

With that, he shuffled the forms again, stamped and gathered them, and handed them to Tesfai. "Welcome to the United States!" His cheerfulness translated to the whole group, even those less comfortable with the language. "You are now officially cleared to live in America."

Tesfai thanked the officer, and guided his family toward the exit. Tomorrow they would board one more plane for what they thought was their final stop, Washington D.C.

A NEW FRIEND, AN OLD FRIEND

Tesfai and Abeba shepherded Efrem and Abel off the plane into the bustling crowds of Washington D.C.'s National Airport. They searched for the arrivals area, where they hoped to be united with their sponsoring organization, the Chevy Chase United Methodist Church.

"How will we know them? What do they look like?" Efrem gawked at all the people hurrying along National's corridors. Any one person seemed to have more luggage than the entire Tesema/Gilazgi family.

"How will they ever find us?" Abeba was as concerned as her brother.

She'd noticed the hordes of people spilling into the arrivals waiting area.

Tesfai and his family moved through the door, blinking at the maelstrom of people. He had the name "Chevy Chase United Methodist Church" engraved on his brain. How would the two groups find one another?

Suddenly, he heard shouting. Abeba, too, turned toward the boisterous call. She and Tesfai saw several hands waving, beneath signs proclaiming, "Chevy Chase UMC welcomes the Tesema Family!". One of the waving women dashed over, intent upon hugging Abeba and Tesfai.

"You're here! Welcome! Come meet the rest of the group! I'm Nancy Lanman, one of your sponsors. We're so happy to see you!" Nancy gestured for Tesfai and his family to follow her into a quieter section of the hall where her group, four other smiling Americans, now gathered.

Tesfai finally found his voice. "Thank you for being here to greet us." He was overcome with relief. "We weren't sure you'd recognize us. Did you have pictures?"

"Oh no," responded one of Nancy's companions, another kind-looking woman. "We just knew you were coming from Sudan and that you are Ethiopians. But it wasn't hard to spot you. See, you're the only ones arriving with almost no luggage. And," she added mischievously, "not only are you carrying big tags saying you are part of the refugee program, but most people don't show up in the middle of our winter without warm coats."

"Which we now present to you!" Nancy laughed. "We figured coming from Sudan—we've done our research—you would not be prepared for our cold winter. We just hope the coats fit; you're all so thin."

"Were you affected by the famine in Ethiopia?" asked one of the men in the group. "Our church has given to the relief efforts there."

Tesfai answered for the group. "No, we were just too poor to buy much food. We often went hungry while living in Sudan. But we were still very happy because we were allowed to serve the Lord."

Nancy smiled. "I am pleased to tell you, that here you will be able to serve the Lord and eat!"

One of the men finally spoke. "So, you have your coats on. Obviously, not much luggage to carry. We're ready to take you to the apartment we've prepared for you. Shall we go?"

Nancy's enthusiasm bubbled. "It'll be like a parade! We couldn't get all of us in one car, so we have three cars to accommodate you and all our welcome group members. Let's go!" She waved everyone on. The group of nine started out of the airport building toward the parking garage.

Suddenly, their procession was interrupted by a shout of amazement coming from the taxi line. "Tesfai! Tesfai!"

Everyone turned, staring at the young man running in their direction, waving his arms madly. They noticed his taxi driver uniform, then the yellow cab left double parked at the arrivals level access road, driver's door standing open.

"Tesfai, is it really you? The young Ethiopian man rushed up, nearly out of breath from excitement. "Excuse me, everyone, I'm sorry, but Tesfai, it's you, isn't it? I'm Fikeru!"

"Fikeru!" Tesfai's jaw dropped. "From Djibouti! How did you get here? We've just arrived. See, I'm with my wife and son, and here is Efrem, Abeba's brother. And these people," Tesfai indicated the group, "are our wonderful sponsors from Chevy Chase United Methodist Church."

The group didn't know what to say. Fikeru took advantage of the lull. "Say, Tesfai, I've got to run—er—drive off. I'm a taxi driver. But here." He fumbled with a pen and paper. "Here is my phone number. You must call me!" He pushed the paper at Tesfai, gave him a clap on the back, waved cheerfully to the group, and jumped back into his car.

Nancy was the first to speak. "Tesfai, you haven't been in Washington D.C. for even an hour, and already someone knows you?"

Tesfai shook his head. He looked toward Abeba, who knew his dissolute lifestyle in Djibouti. "I think God just found me my first job!"

NOT IN KHARTOUM ANYMORE

"Tesfai, we're no longer in Khartoum, are we?" Abeba looked around the apartment. Nancy Lanman and the rest of her welcome group had brought them to their new home in Silver Springs, MD. Located in a cluster of multi-story buildings at the intersection of 16th Ave and Eastwest Highway, their apartment looked out onto walkways that connected the buildings to the street.

"Look!" Sixteen-year-old Efrem peered out the window. "Guys my age!" He gestured toward young men sauntering along the sidewalk, boom boxes hoisted on their shoulders. Abeba and Tesfai glanced at one another, cautiously.

Nancy and the group showed the Ethiopian family the ways they'd prepared for their arrival. "You'll see that the refrigerator is full! We probably failed to get food you might be used to, but we can show you later where the grocery stores are."

Tesfai hoped his gratefulness was translating to the group. "Food is food. We are used to going without, so anything is a blessing. I am sure whatever you've provided we will love!"

"Don't forget," said one of the other women in the group, "there's also food in the cupboards. And plates, and cups and silverware, and cooking equipment."

"Say," asked one of the men. "Do you know how to use a can opener? Or a coffee maker?" He gestured to the coffee maker sitting on the counter. "How about working the stove?"

Tesfai was amazed at all the gadgets. "We'll manage. You kind people have thought of everything! By the way, did you know Ethiopia is famous for its coffee? We'll get some soon and prove why!" Everyone chuckled.

"So here is the TV," said Nancy, pointing to a square box on a table in the living room. "The election for president is coming up later this year; it'll be President Reagan running for reelection."

"You'll notice we have the beds made. And the towels and stuff for the bathroom," said another person. "We kind of figured Efrem would get his own room—you've got two bedrooms here, so that's possible."

Efrem stuck his head into one of the bedrooms. "Wow, I've never had my own room!"

Tesfai explained the teen's excitement. "We've always shared living quarters. Part of it is cultural, but mainly it's because space is limited.

This is more room than we've ever had as a married couple!"

"We are deeply grateful to you," added Abeba. "Our hope is to make you and the rest of America as happy to have us here as we are to be here."

Nancy spoke for the group. "And now, I think it's time for us to leave you alone to explore the apartment and neighborhood. Do be a little careful about going out at night. And don't get lost! Until you get used to being here, all the buildings may look alike." With that, she and her jovial group offered hugs and promises to visit later; then they left the immigrants alone.

Abeba and Tesfai stood quietly, watching their benefactors walking toward their waiting cars. Abeba repeated her original observation: "We are not in Khartoum anymore."

"No, we're finally in America. We're finally here!"

"What will God have us do now?" They were dazed by their new surroundings and the kindness of the Chevy Chase church.

"Perhaps," Abeba suggested, "we should start by eating some of this very interesting food from America!"

A SURPRISING PHONE
CONVERSATION

"I need to call Fikeru." Tesfai wasn't sure he was ready for that conversation. "Now that we have a phone, I want to see how he fared in Djibouti after I left, and how he got to America."

"What will you say?" Abeba wanted to help if she could. "Do you think he'll be receptive to your new life? Neither of you knew Jesus when you were living in Djibouti."

"Surviving in Djibouti, you mean." Tesfai remembered that old life. "Well, to start, I suppose I'll tell him how the church people have cared for us these last couple of weeks. I'll tell him about you and how we met, how we were prayer partners and then friends and now married. I can tell him about our time in Jeddah and Khartoum."

"Any of those would be good openings to talk about your new life. I'm going to start praying for your phone conversation; I'll be here, praying that God will use you as an evangelist once again!"

"As soon as I realized it was Fikeru running toward us, I marveled about how God works. Surely God brought us in contact so

I can tell Fikeru about Jesus." Tesfai went into the next room and dialed the number Fikeru had thrust at him.

Abeba prayed: "Dear Heavenly Father, please bless Tesfai's ministry to Fikeru. May Fikeru be open to hearing about You, and may he come to know the love of Your dear Son Jesus." Abeba was still praying when she heard Tesfai's exclamation from the other room.

"Praise the Lord! Fikeru, my brother in Christ! God is truly an awesome God!"

Abeba rushed into the room. She found Tesfai jumping up and down. Then Tesfai hung up the phone and grabbed Abeba. "Fikeru is a believer!"

"How can that be? That fast?" Abeba fairly stumbled over her words.

"No! Not because of me! Fikeru came to the Lord after he arrived in the States! Abeba, here's the funny thing—when Fikeru saw me, he was thinking he needed to tell me about Jesus, and I was thinking the same thing about him. We talked about this and that, and then when I finally told him I'd met my wife in church and that we were prayer partners, that's when we discovered we are both believers!"

"Amazing!" Abeba smiled broadly. "So where does he go to church?"

"Fikeru told me there is an Ethiopian church meeting every Sunday afternoon in Washington, D.C. at 19th and H streets. About twenty-five people attend. He told me how we can take the Metro to get there—I think we know how to do that now—and we're invited! Fikeru said the Ethiopian population is growing here and around the country since so many are fleeing the civil war; thousands are being accepted as refugees from the Derg government." Tesfai smiled at Abeba. "We're going to meet other Ethiopian Christians!"

"But aren't we part of the Chevy Chase UMC church? Don't we owe them our loyalty?" Abeba was torn.

"We can do both! We will stay involved with the UMC church. They've welcomed us, not just as refugees but as part of their church family. In the afternoon, we can join the Ethiopian community." Tesfai bubbled with excitement.

Abeba was convinced. "Just think, we've only been here two weeks. Already we've gained weight, started to learn about American politics, and made friends in two churches!"

It's a good life." Tesfai sighed. "I wonder if we're supposed to just enjoy this good life, or if there is more for us to do?"

AN OVERHEARD
CONVERSATION

Abeba was sipping her mid-morning coffee watching the crowd of Ethiopians milling around her in small groups. Shortly after they began attending Fikeru's church, she and Tesfai had been invited to a conference of Ethiopian Christians at the Mennonite Conference Center in Lancaster, PA. In the mid-1980s the network of Ethiopians was incorporating new arrivals and spreading across the United States and into Canada. This was one such gathering.

Abeba put down her coffee and tuned in to an animated conversation between two women at the table next to her.

"I tell you, Rahel, there was this sister arrested in Saudi Arabia for being a Christian!"

"Just for being a Christian? Oh, come on, Fikirte. How did they discover her? What happened?"

"I think she and her friend got caught witnessing to Muslim women. They took them to jail, and their husbands had to figure out how to get them out. And get this: the women were pregnant!"

"And?" prompted Rahel.

"Apparently all of them were kicked out of Saudi Arabia and sent to Sudan! People have been killed in Saudi Arabia for less." The one called Fikirte clasped her hands together. "God saved the women, and then they all went to Sudan and preached some more. They helped plant a bunch of churches in Sudan."

"How do you know all this?"

"I have a friend in Ethiopia who heard it from her cousin in Saudi Arabia, who has a friend or a brother-in-law or something in Sudan, and then that person said these people—the ones who got deported from Saudi Arabia—have now come to the United States!"

"Imagine going through all that and still evangelizing. I wonder how they coped in Sudan, and what are they doing now? Do you suppose Melese Wogu knows about this? Maybe he can find these people, wherever they are, and have them tell their story at the next conference." Melese Wogu, the conference organizer, was a leader within the Mennonite Ethiopian Christian community.

Abeba turned toward the women. "I couldn't help but overhear your discussion. I can help you find the people you are talking about."

Fikirte's eyes lit up. "Really? What a blessing that would be! Do you know their names? Where are they now? We'd love to meet them!"

"Abeba," said Abeba. "And Tesfai. I am Abeba, and Tesfai is my husband. I believe we are the ones you're looking for. Along with our friends Elsa and Fitsum."

The women stared at Abeba. "You've got to meet Melese Wogu! He will want you to share your story, I know it!"

Abeba nodded. "My husband, Tesfai, is one of the most sociable men you'll ever meet. I have a feeling he's already met Melese. Earlier this morning, in fact, Tesfai was telling me about someone asking him to share about our time in Sudan."

"And what will you do now that you're here in the States?"

"This we are still figuring out. With God's help, we will find the answer. Right now, we are just grateful to be alive and here. I can tell you that the United States is definitely different from anywhere else we've lived!"

Fikirte agreed. "It will be interesting where God will take you next. For you can be sure that God has a plan." No one was more sure than Abeba, except, maybe, Tesfai, who was, at that moment, getting an inkling of God's plan.

DESPAIR, ENCOURAGEMENT, A CLUE

Tesfai had concluded his talk at the Mennonite Conference Center. As Abeba's two women companions had guessed, Melese Wogu indeed had been keen for him to address the gathering and share his and Abeba's miraculous experiences in Saudi Arabia and Sudan. As Tesfai walked away from the podium, and as the crowd broke for dinner, a man rushed up to him.

"Do you remember me?"

Tesfai was startled, then he broke into a wide grin. He clasped the man's hand. "Samuel! One of the brothers from the Sudanese ministry! What a fantastic surprise!" Tesfai took Samuel's hand and pulled him along.

"Abeba, come over! It's our brother Samuel!"

Abeba recognized Samuel immediately. "Samuel, it's so good to see you again. We heard you had come to the States a few months before we did. How are you doing? Where are you living? How did you get here? And how is it we have been at this conference two days and just now we have met you again?"

Abeba knew the Ethiopian Christian gathering was large, but it wasn't that large. She and Tesfai should have bumped into their friend sooner.

"I only came to the meeting this one day." Samuel's eyes were cast down.

"It was my last hope."

"Last hope? Last hope for what?" Tesfai was puzzled.

Samuel started crying, shoulders heaving. Tesfai and Abeba eased him into a nearby chair away from curious onlookers. "What's wrong?" asked Abeba, softly.

"My life, it's no use, I can't get used to this country!" Samuel finally stopped weeping enough to speak. "I'm through! I just want to kill myself. It's been too hard living here!"

Tesfai breathed a silent prayer. "But you're here at this conference, where we're reminded of God's love and His plan for our lives. That is why you are here, Samuel. The Lord brought us here for a reason." Tesfai was trying to understand Samuel's distress.

"Yes, I am here. I thought perhaps it would be good to see my countrymen one more time before I killed myself. And, to ask God to forgive me for being so weak."

"Weak?" asked Abeba.

"I was so relieved to get permission to come to the United States, but it's been hard living here! Everything, it was too easy, like getting food and being free to move about and going to church without anyone bothering me. Now my refugee support is running out. I haven't been able to find a job. I feel God has abandoned me. God must hate me! I am weak; I can't fit into this country." His tears flowed freely "But then I saw you talking up there. I listened. I remembered our good times sharing the Gospel in Sudan."

Tesfai remembered well. "Those were good, but hard times. They came at a cost. Hunger, for example. Homelessness. Religious persecution.

God used you then; God can use you now."

"It's the circumstances that have changed," Abeba added. "You are still a child of God."

"My brother, remember that Jesus always cares for the weak and the hurting. I don't think you are weak, but I know you are hurting. Let us pray with you and for you!"

Samuel nodded, then bowed his head as Tesfai and Abeba prayed. He stayed silent, occasionally releasing heavy sighs.

Abeba began to close their prayer "And keep Samuel always in Your care, as he is Your precious child."

"We pray all this in Jesus's name. Amen," concluded Tesfai. He and Abeba continued holding Samuel's hands and stayed silent for several minutes.

Finally, Samuel murmured, "You have given me some hope. I will keep trying."

Tesfai stood in front of Samuel, looked him in the eye, and said, "God has given you hope. We are only the instruments. And yes, keep trying. You are in God's care. God loves you! That, my friend, is why you are here."

"Do you have a phone?" asked Abeba. "We would be happy to stay in touch for as long as you need."

Samuel and the Tesemas exchanged phone numbers. Samuel accepted a hug from Tesfai and Abeba. "I need to go now, but I will never forget how God must have arranged this meeting!"

"Now you sound like the Samuel I remember."

Abeba took Samuel's hand in her hands. "Go with God's blessing and remember, we are only a phone call away!"

Abeba and Tesfai were moved by the encounter. Abeba spoke first. "I think maybe God is pointing us in the direction of new ministry."

Tesfai agreed. "Not just saving new souls, but encouraging those who are refugees and already believers. The immigration officer may have been wrong. There is still a need for missionaries in America!"

NOW WHAT?

"Abeba, I'm wondering ..." Tesfai began tentatively. Efrem was in the next room watching MTV; Abel was playing in the corner of the kitchen. He had discovered that a large pot and a spatula made a good drum set.

Tesfai and Abeba were relaxing after supper.

"I've seen you gaze off in space a lot lately. What are you thinking?"

"We've been here almost five months. Life is good, we can eat, and we never have to worry about that. We've got a TV and a phone, and we've found the grocery stores and the clothing stores. We have a small bank account and well, life is comfortable."

"Too comfortable?" Abeba had a sense of where her husband was going with the conversation. "I've wondered the same. I love our life here. We get to be part of two churches. We've made friends, and we've been hosting a wonderful Bible study here in our apartment, with Anglos and Ethiopians, together. We've adjusted well to life in America. We have our ministry of encouraging the believers, Yet ..."

"I fear we are getting complacent. We're people who believe there is more to life than being comfortable. I was talking to my cousin Emmanuel on the phone. He agrees with Nancy and the pastor of our Chevy Chase church."

"About?"

"They all think I should get a regular job. Emmanuel's offered to buy me a taxi. Of course, I want to work, and you know that soon the financial support we have been receiving from the UMC church will run out. But I keep thinking—get a job and stay here with ministry as a sort of hobby, or make ministry the central part of our lives?"

Abeba agreed. "Like in Sudan. We were always busy with ministry, doing home Bible studies and group meetings. You spent most of your time training evangelists and church leaders to start new churches. We brought people to Jesus and helped them in their faith walk. Do you suppose we simply miss being in the middle of things? Here we're involved, but it's different. There's lots of ministry going on that we haven't started, ministry that we're not leading. Is it about God or about us?"

"I've thought about that." Tesfai continued. "I keep remembering the time with BJ and Mark in Jeddah. I remember how we were invited to join Berhanu, Melaku and Tesfa in planting churches in Sudan. I wonder if full-time ministry is supposed to be our calling, although I am not sure what that would look like in America."

"There's one way to find out. Bring it to the Lord in prayer. Ask for prayers at our Bible study. If this is God's plan, we will get the answer in the form of an affirmation! If not, that is all right. We have always trusted the Lord to lead."

Both began to pray, and to wonder where God would lead. The answer did not take long to come, an answer their friends found most surprising.

MOVING FORWARD, AND AGAIN

"**B**ut how would you do this? Where would you go?"
Abeba and Tesfai had shared their dilemma with their mid-week Bible study. Their friends were cautiously supportive of their hopes to pursue full-time ministry.

"We're still figuring out those details. There's a place to study, just outside of Tulsa. Abeba reminded me of a magazine our church in Jeddah used to get, Word of Faith. It's put out by the Rhema Bible Training Center, located in Broken Arrow, Oklahoma."

"Neither Tesfai nor I have ever had any formal Bible instruction." Abeba filled in the details. "We were thinking that, while we did Gospel work in Saudi Arabia and Sudan without training, here in the States it would be worthwhile to have formal instruction. If we learn more, we can share more!"

One of the group members reflected aloud. "It could work. Have you contacted this Rhema place?"

"Actually, we did. We called and wrote. I don't think they get too many Ethiopian applicants." Tesfai laughed. "But they have accepted us; they have invited us to come to study at their school."

154

"We're praying about this, as you can imagine. Living in the Tulsa area would be a change for us, that is for sure." She looked at her young brother. "My concern is, how will Efrem cope?"

Tesfai jumped in: "Efrem's a good kid. He'll make friends. Anyway, we'll be with him to guide him. Teenagers can adapt. Although we will have to make an extra effort to keep an eye on him." Tesfai remembered his teen years, hoping Efrem wouldn't face the same temptations.

"You have all been so good to us here. All of you!" Abeba gestured to both Anglo and Ethiopian members of the group. "It would be so easy to stay here, work and keep on as we are doing. We're happy, and life is good."

Tesfai continued Abeba's comments: "But we think there is more we could be doing. Which is why we've been praying and searching for God's will. We are asking for your advice. And your blessing."

Nancy was the first to speak. "Our pastor once said that God's leading is a little like an itch you have to scratch. You're happy, life is good, you've got a network for employment and fellowship here. But you've also got this itch toward full-time Gospel work. Your itch is never going to go away."

Peggy, another faithful member from the Chevy Chase UMC, joined the conversation. "If you are being called to full-time ministry, God will not leave you alone until you answer the call. Think of Jonah! Well, maybe not Jonah; he kept running from God's calling. You're not running, but you get the picture. I believe God will keep after you and find a way for you to do this!"

Abeba smiled. "That's what we concluded. Just like when we left Eritrea and Ethiopia, Saudi Arabia and Sudan, we are prepared to leave here. Even though it will be hard, leaving such dear friends as you have been to us."

"I plan to work and go to school," said Tesfai. "We'll be tentmakers.

Like St. Paul!"

"Even St. Paul accepted help from other believers. Like from the Philippians." Peggy spoke for the group. "Let our group pray with you.

But also let us be your Philippians."

"We did not expect you to give us money!" Tesfai exclaimed in agitation. "We only want your prayers and your blessing! You have already been too generous to us."

"You certainly have our blessing, and you shall have our prayers. However, Bible schools cost money. Consider any help we—and UMC—can offer as an investment. An investment toward furthering the Gospel." Nancy and the others nodded their assent.

Peggy explained. "It's easy to say we'll pray and even to say we give our blessing. Helping pay your tuition means we take your calling seriously. God put this in your hearts. It is clear God has great plans for you. We are only the instruments of God's will."

Abeba and Tesfai looked at one another in disbelief, then turned toward the study participants.

"When Abeba and I first wondered about this, we resolved to pray and to consult with you regarding our intent."

His wife picked up the story. "We felt that if God meant for us to work toward full-time ministry, it would be affirmed through you, our dear sisters and brothers in Christ."

"God has spoken through you." Tesfai knew the emotion showed on his face. "Thank you from the bottom of our hearts!"

No one would have guessed, though, how great the difficulties would be for an Ethiopian missionary family navigating middle America.

CHALLENGES

B y 1986 the Tesemas had been in Oklahoma for two good years. But then the trouble started.

"Tesfai, we have some challenges we need to face," Abeba told her husband one morning. "We need to talk and pray. Pray a lot. I know how busy you are, but I need you to find time for this."

Tesfai was about to head out the door for classes at Rhema Bible Training Center. One glance at Abeba's face was enough to convince him otherwise. "I'll skip today's session. I can make up the work."

Tesfai remembered the last time Abeba had to speak her mind, when they lived in Sudan. He had been busy and absent from his family. "Let's talk. Or rather, you talk, and I'll listen. Do you want me to hold Daniel?" Daniel was the couple's second son, born in June 1985. Abel was playing in the next room.

Abeba took a deep breath. "You're doing everything you have to do at school and at work. You go to classes in the morning, you work at McDonalds in the afternoon, and in between you are the janitor at the local public school. You have taken two jobs to support us, and you're involved in ministry in ways we would never have imagined in Washington, D.C."

"You're hinting I'm not around very much, aren't you? The reasons may be good, but I'm still not around."

"Yes, this is a problem even if the reasons are good. I do love that God has started using you to help the church. The extensive network Ethiopians have developed in the U.S. has allowed us to be a blessing to many."

Tesfai agreed. "It was a blessing that Pastor Zeleke in Dallas heard about me—a new guy—taking classes in Oklahoma. The Dallas Ethiopian church has been growing, and has helped start churches around the country. But this is also a problem for you, isn't it? Not just a blessing."

"Yes." Abeba felt a familiar tug of longing. "I'm caring for two young boys. Then there is my brother, Efrem; Tesfai, if you'd been around more you would have noticed—Efrem is struggling."

"I have noticed he's lost a little energy," responded Tesfai. "What is going on?"

"There are almost no Ethiopians in Tulsa. Just us and Fitsum and Elsa and their little kids. But more than that, he's having trouble in school. The school in Broken Arrow is nearly all white, and they don't know what to do with a new kid who is black—as they say—and still learning English. Efrem's been called names, he's been told he's lazy, he's been disciplined for things he didn't do, and he's miserable. I can barely get him to go to school."

"Isn't he in school now?" asked Tesfai, tentatively.

"Yes. I told him last night that I would discuss his situation with you, and we would try to find a solution. He's a good kid, and he wants an education—but being miserable at school is a high price to pay."

Tesfai summed up his wife's dilemma. "You're at your wits' end with Efrem, and you're feeling isolated caring for Abel and Daniel. And I'm not here to help."

Abeba nodded. "I've been thinking about this, a lot. I do not resent you taking classes while I am not. I can see that in our church environment they expect the man to be the leader, so for you to go to Dallas, or anywhere else, to be a church leader and then to train other leaders makes sense. Although more of these Americans should see the blessings women leaders can bring to mission work.

"Your classes allow you to make connections for ministry opportunities, and I understand that, too. It's just, well, I'm lonely. With you gone so much, and me isolated, this is just the kind of situation that could destroy our marriage."

Tesfai was convinced by Abeba's assessment, but he needed to sort out the issues. "Let's tackle one at a time. The first thing is to get Efrem into a better situation. We have good friends in Washington D.C. Maybe one of the Chevy Chase UMC families would take him in? He was happy in Washington, and the UMC families liked having him around."

"A promising idea." Abeba's face registered some relief. "I'll tell Efrem tonight. He'll miss us, but I think he'll thrive again in D.C."

Tesfai felt like the plan was unfolding before him as he spoke. "My two years of study are almost over. How about you start classes when I finish? Classes start again in early 1987. You can attend school in the morning, and I'll take care of the boys. I'll still work in the afternoons. I can drop the McDonald's job and keep the janitor job in the school district. I'm about to get a small raise, and that job provides us with health insurance. Every other weekend I can go to Dallas to work alongside Pastor Zeleke planting new churches. Southwest Airlines has this great fare right now, $19 one way between Tulsa and Dallas, which we can afford! What do you think?"

"I accept your ideas." Abeba smiled. "We find Efrem a better situation, you keep the weekend ministry in Dallas, I get to go to school in a few months. Maybe I'll even make a friend!"

"I want us to be a team. Even if the Americans expect the man to take the lead, I still see you as my equal partner! I promise to respect and treat you as such."

"I know it's our circumstances that have been the problem. I believe that with talking and praying and action, we will thrive here. God has brought us too far to fail us now!" The next phase of life in America would be the proof of the veracity of Abeba's words.

AND GOD SAID, "GO WEST..."

"Abeba, I have news," said Tesfai. It was the summer of 1989. "News?" Abeba wasn't sure she was prepared for Tesfai's 'news'.

"An opportunity if you agree."

The couple sat in the kitchen. Six-year-old Abel and four-year-old Daniel were laughing at kiddie cartoons on TV.

Tesfai began slowly. "When I was in Dallas last time, Pastor Zeleke told me he'd accepted a call to an Ethiopian congregation in Denver. They want a pastor out there to help grow the church."

"Are we being asked to move to Dallas?"

"No. Pastor Zeleke is being replaced by Pastor Seifu, whom he's known for several years. I've met Pastor Seifu. He'll do a respectable job."

"Okay. What's the opportunity you want me to think about?"

"Pastor Seifu is leaving San Jose, California to go to Dallas. In 1987 he started a congregation in San Jose called the Ethiopian Christian Fellowship. It's small. Pastor Zeleke has suggested they call me to be its pastor once Pastor Seifu leaves for Dallas. What do you think?"

"I'm wondering why all the switching around. Why not just call you to Dallas? Or Denver? Not that I don't want to move to San Jose! After all, Elsa and Fitsum are there and, come to think of it, we were planning to go to San Jose as part of our vacation. But now we may get to live there.

What's with all the switches?"

"Pastor Zeleke explained to me that Denver and Dallas are now established churches. They've gotten over the new church hurdle, and they want help growing membership. Pastor Zeleke says my gift is raising up churches, and finding leaders and ministers for new congregations. Remember all the churches we planted in Sudan?

"All the leaders you trained, the outreach you did." Abeba's smile of remembrance lit the room.

"It seems that kind of work can be done here as well," said Tesfai. "Many American churches don't seem to know how to do this. American churches do not have a missionary culture; most see ministry as taking care of current members. What we bring to the church here is valuable."

Abeba agreed but was not convinced a move was good. Tesfai's next words were the strongest part of his argument.

"The Ethiopian Christian Fellowship in San Jose is looking for someone like me to do it. It would be a full-time ministry position. My job would be to strengthen the church, raise leaders, and do outreach into the Ethiopian community. There aren't that many Ethiopians in San Jose yet, but that is changing. The ECF wants to support new Ethiopian arrivals in the area. They want to offer a Christian home for worship and fellowship."

"Full-time ministry. Your dream. We sort of did this in Sudan."

"Except in Sudan we didn't have the Bible knowledge we have now, and we were doing our work informally. This time, we have Bible training. It's a formal call, which means the congregation is committing to support us, even as we commit to supporting them in their church life and to growing churches elsewhere."

Abeba laughed. "Another difference, I suppose, is that we will not have to worry about going hungry. I agree. We should do this; after all, it's why we came to Broken Arrow and the Bible training center, following God's lead."

"You will miss your friends." Tesfai took Abeba's hands in his. "You've made good friends these last few years."

"Yes, when I figured out how to collect furniture from empty apartments and share it with new tenants who need furniture I met Sheila, Chantay, and Teresa. I will never forget Stephanie, my best friend! Remember how she couldn't believe we never locked our doors because we didn't do that in Sudan? Who knew that an Anglo woman and an Eritrean woman could become such fast friends! We talked about everything, prayed, and studied together. Yes, I will miss everyone, but especially Stephanie."

"Grace Church in Broken Arrow, wants to ordain me before we leave for San Jose. It's their way of recognizing ECF's call to ministry and confirming my ministry gifts. It'll be a celebration! I invite you to come!"

"Very funny. What you're really asking is, will I bring food to the party. That would also be a 'yes'. Now, how am I going to tell my friends about this? It seems whenever God leads, we always end up moving. And then, we get to tell the boys they are going on a really long trip!"

"Where they will meet other Ethiopian kids. Just think, another adventure! I think we and our boys will enjoy the ECF! Just consider all the possibilities!" Tesfai was ready for the next step.

He just didn't know all the steps that would follow.

A BIG STEP!

In 1989 the family made the move to San Jose, a move God blessed. The Ethiopian Christian Fellowship prospered. New members were added. New ministries began. But by 1997 several challenges loomed for the church, and for the Tesemas.

"Why?" demanded an ECF elder. "Why must you go on to seminary? You've done excellent work here these last eight years. Our church has grown, and you've gotten your Bachelor's degree. Why do you want more education?"

"Have you become too good for us?" A second elder chimed in. "Remember, we are a church in the Pentecostal tradition. We don't require our ministers to have extensive schooling. Love of Scripture is enough! Your B.A. in Bible and Theology is plenty! We called you for your evangelism experience, and you certainly know the Bible. Why must you take time away to go to school again?"

Tesfai addressed the group of skeptical elders patiently. "I am grateful that you approved my B.A. studies, and I am indeed proud to have attained this college degree. However, I didn't do this for me. I wanted the schooling so I could be a better pastor. I feel the same about pursuing the Master's in Divinity. In the United States, this degree is considered the minimum one needs to be a credible pastor."

"Are you so Americanized that you must adhere to this ... this ... this credible pastor business?" The first elder was scoffing now. "What about us? And our church? We've grown, I tell you, without your extra so-called education. Maybe we've grown despite you running off to school!" He leaned back in his chair, fixing Tesfai with a belligerent stare.

Tesfai resisted the impulse to sigh. "Remember, please, that I got my B.A. on my own time. I was and still am your full-time pastor. No one at ECF suffered, since I went to school and studied at night. I've worked out a similar schedule for the seminary. I did not take time away from the ECF for my B.A. nor will I take time away for the M.Div."

"I can confirm this." Another elder tried to sooth the fears. "You served us full-time during your B.A. studies. You performed baptisms and weddings; you counseled couples before and after their marriages; and you've stayed keen to raise up leaders in our church. Some of us sitting here," he glanced about the room, "are among those you trained. Our membership has grown from fewer than thirty members to 200 regular worshippers. And this does not count the people who just come and go. With all this success, why the need for another degree? Even if you do use your own time to get it? Just to be like the Americans?"

Tesfai took a deep breath. "Yes, we've grown. By God's grace, we have grown. God has been good to us. But I believe there are a couple of things we ignore at our peril. First, consider what's been happening in Ethiopia, and how it will affect us."

"The Derg is gone! Thank God for that!" exclaimed one of the elders.

Tesfai agreed. "Yes, the Derg is gone. And yes, that is a blessing. But with its demise we have a new reality. Before 1991 the only Christian leaders willing to oppose the Derg publicly were Protestants: Pentecostals, Lutherans, Baptists, and so forth. Orthodox and Catholics church hierarchies were willing to work with the Derg, as they did with Emperor Haile Selassie."

"So?"

"So even though church members of all faiths fled Ethiopia, Orthodox priests did not leave. That has helped ECF. Ethiopians in our area who wanted to worship God came to ECF. We became a center for other Ethiopians as well, since new arrivals looked for familiarity from back home. Some of these new arrivals became believers, thanks to ECF's evangelism."

"Now the Derg is gone ..." said an elder, thoughtfully.

"The government that took down the Derg also took over the Orthodox church. It fired its Patriarch and brought in a new guy. That would be like the Italian government firing the Pope!

"So, Orthodox priests have been leaving Ethiopia and coming to the United States, citing religious persecution. Many have been organizing and building Orthodox churches. We lost some members to these Orthodox congregations. Newly arrived Ethiopians now have a choice."

"You're suggesting we now have limited capacity to grow?" The elders seemed to understand.

"Sort of. We're no longer the only Ethiopian church in the area and that's affected our ability to reach out to new arrivals."

"You think your M.Div. will fix this?"

"It gives us more credibility, but that's not the only reason. There is another problem that we face. It's what to do about the kids."

"The kids?" The elders seemed puzzled. "The kids come to church with us. They grow up, they keep their Ethiopian culture and our beliefs. They keep going to church here. What's to do about the kids?"

"I don't think it's as easy as that. I have two boys. If anyone can bring their kids up in the faith here at ECF, it would be me and

Abeba—we're ministers!" Tesfai liked to emphasize that he and Abeba were partners in the Gospel. "But here's the thing. While adults at ECF are firm in their beliefs and imbued with Ethiopian culture, they also lack confidence and training to teach the next generation. We're not accustomed to teaching Sunday School. And our young people don't get as much out of our worship services as do the adults, because they are not so tied to Ethiopian traditional culture."

"So …"

"We need to think about our future. For our generation—the adults who lived in, left, and now remember Ethiopia—the ECF is a fine well for Christian faith support and evangelism. For our children, this well is insufficient. Abeba and I propose that we become intentional about developing children's and youth ministry."

"Therefore you want an M.Div.? Again, what's wrong with your B.A.?"

"My B.A. was about theological study and Bible content. The M.Div. delves into practical ministry. Listen, my sons are believers. They want to go to church. The only problem is, they have started saying they want to go to their church! They've discovered another church, thanks to their friends, a church they prefer to ECF. Abeba drives them to this new church and will do so until Abel is ready to drive. We think this is better than trying to force them to attend our church."

"Disloyal sons," scoffed one of the elders.

"No, American sons. American offspring, that we have not figured out how to nourish within our ECF structure. That's why I want permission to pursue my M.Div. I want our church to do a better job of reaching the next generation."

"I think you are inventing problems to justify getting another degree. Maybe you don't want to be Ethiopian any more. Like your sons," the elder added, defiantly.

Tesfai looked at him, sadly. "Of course I want to be Ethiopian. I am Ethiopian! As are my sons. But we cannot expect our church to thrive if we refuse to look ahead."

"I say, no M.Div.!" interrupted an elder. "Don't go after any more big ideas! We're fine as we are."

Tesfai was quiet for a moment. "I'm sorry. I must follow where I sense God is leading. Wherever that is, no matter the cost."

"Even if you lose us from the ECF?" challenged an elder. "We could leave, you know."

"If you feel you must leave, that would be very painful. Still, I must follow God's leading. God will provide. God always has."

Tesfai sat heavily in his seat.

GOD STEPS IN AGAIN

The two pastors sat in the office of Lutheran pastor Robert Newton. They shared a love for mission work, both understanding that America was becoming a Christian mission field.

It was 2001. Tesfai had earned his M.Div. degree from the Mennonite Bible Seminary in Fresno, CA. He'd remained full-time as the pastor of the Ethiopian Christian Fellowship, but he and Abeba continued worrying about the church's future. It had a growing contingent of American-born Ethiopian youth, and the young people were not as committed as they could or should be.

Earlier in 2001, Tesfai had a conversation about this with Pastor Zeleke.

"Zeleke, young Ethiopian-Americans are like a whole new mission field! A mission field, I'm afraid, we're not reaching. How do I bridge this gap between our tradition-oriented adults, and our American-acculturated kids?"

Zeleke paused. "I have an Ethiopian pastor friend who might be able to help. He has a different church background, but he is wise. Call Pastor Yohannes Mengsteab in St. Louis, He's Eritrean, a Lutheran, and a pastor. He knows about missions; he's the Director of New Church Development for the Lutheran Church Missouri

Synod. He works for another pastor, Dr. Bob Scudieri, who is also keen on missions. And you, as you have said, have a mission to pursue."

"Lutheran, eh? That is different from our background. I remember, the Lutheran church was a presence in Ethiopia when I was growing up. I always figured they were sort of like a Protestant Orthodox church."

"Well, Yohannes can tell you more, of course, but Lutherans are really big on Sunday School and faith training. And on lay leadership."

"The sorts of things I'm trying to do at ECF."

"So, call him! Pastor Yohannes works in the mission field, helping plant new churches. I'm sure you would find him supportive. He probably knows people in the San Jose area who can work with you."

So it was that on this day Pastor Tesfai was sitting with Pastor Bob Newton, friend of Pastor Yohannes Mengsteab, friend of Pastor Zeleke.

"It seems to me that you have identified a mission field," said Pastor Newton. "Yours is a dilemma, in fact, faced by many American congregations, not just Ethiopian churches."

"I keep thinking of a well," said Tesfai. "I was reading, the other day, about Jesus and the Samaritan woman. It struck me that I have access to a wonderful well of faith support and encouragement. But the next generation, including my children, can't quite access that same well. Something is getting in the way, and I think it's differing cultural perspectives."

"That is the epitome of cross-cultural ministry," suggested Bob. "And cross-cultural can relate to different ethnic groups and different generations. Tesfai, first we need to acknowledge there is a problem, which you have done!"

"Yes, though I have had a slight difference of opinion with my congregation regarding this."

"You wouldn't be alone." Bob reassured his new friend. "Tesfai, I have something for you to consider. Actually, a couple of somethings. You're a pastor. Why not join the Lutheran church as a Lutheran pastor? You've certainly got the heart. We in the LCMS have a program that can provide you with more doctrinal background and practical education, and a process for initiating you into our Lutheran pastoral ministry.

"The second idea is for you to consider getting your doctorate in missions. Specifically, to study cross-cultural ministry and this issue of outreach to future generations."

"Could I do that here?" asked Tesfai. "They both sound appealing, though I'd want to consult with my wife first. Abeba and I are partners, and I trust her judgment fully."

"Yes, you must talk with Abeba, but no, the doctorate at least you must pursue elsewhere. I recommend attending our Lutheran seminary in Ft. Wayne, IN. It's got a strong mission component. I can make inquiries on your behalf. If you go, though, plan on being in Ft. Wayne for three years, at least. Doctorates take a while to complete!"

"What would my father think?" Tesfai wondered aloud. "I was practically a high school dropout in Ethiopia. And now, here I have a B.A., an M.Div., and maybe in a few years, a doctorate? Not to mention a loving wife, two great sons and a life of pastoral ministry!" Tesfai shook his head in gratitude and amazement.

"Tesfai, remember what Jesus said: 'One who is forgiven much, loves much'. Clearly, God has his eye on you and has from the beginning, even if all this seems like an accident." Pastor Newton leaned forward,

"You are one of God's missionaries, I'm sure of it!"

Tesfai laughed gently. "Now to see if Abeba agrees with your assessment, especially the Ft. Wayne part."

A DIFFERENCE OF OPINION

"Abeba, there is a problem in San Jose." They'd been living in Ft. Wayne ever since Abeba had agreed Tesfai should pursue a doctorate in missions at Lutheran Church Missouri Synod's Concordia Theological Seminary.

"Tell me more," Abeba encouraged.

A number of events had taken place as a result of Tesfai's conversation with Bob Newton. In 2002 they'd joined the LCMS. Tesfai then became a Lutheran pastor, which opened doors for the church and his ministry.

He worked on committees that were interested in second-generation ministries. There he met Pastor Mike Gibson of Mt. Olive Church. After realizing they were kindred spirits in ministry, the pastors had agreed to have ECF and Mt. Olive become sister churches in ministry to Anglo and Ethiopian believers, as well as the broader community.

Various ECF leaders had joined the partnership and, thanks to the help of Rev. Bryce Jessup, they'd successfully attended Jessup's San Jose Bible College. These leaders became pastors at ECF under Tesfai's supervision.

Though this merger had been in the works, it was also one that Tesfai knew was falling apart. He explained it to Abeba.

"The coming together would have had a lot of benefits. Anglos and Ethiopians would learn from each other, and with the dual languages and a larger pool of youth, both Anglo and Ethiopian kids would have more opportunities for faith development and fellowship. With greater numbers and enthusiasm and with the support of the larger Lutheran church, we would evangelize further into the community!"

"So, um, the problem?" reminded Abeba.

"The problem. When I went to San Jose to check on ECF's ministry, the two pastors we left in place told me they'd decided the ECF was not prepared to go through with the vision."

"Why not?"

"They told me it would be too much change for the congregation. They feel the ECF is better off limiting its ministry and outreach to Ethiopians.

They want to keep Ethiopian culture at the center."

Abeba was beginning to understand. "What about the youth; like, for example, our boys? They are not so invested in Ethiopian tradition."

"I asked about that. Apparently, it's not a concern for them. So my assistant pastors and I have a fundamental disagreement regarding the direction of ECF. I am still the senior pastor, but I'm here and not there. The leadership at ECF respects me, but they've declined to follow my vision—our vision—the one we worked on together before you and I left." Tesfai tried to contain his sense of betrayal and disappointment.

Abeba took her husband's hands. "Tesfai, you have often been out in front with a vision of ministry. Of course, we believe it's God's leading and God's plan. But even if it is God's plan, it takes time for everyone else to hear God's voice as quickly as you seem to hear it.

"You and I have been through many changes and challenges. We're used to adapting when we feel the Spirit calling us in new directions. Maybe the other members at ECF, and the pastors, want someplace in their lives where there is not so much change. It's hard being immigrants! Maybe they long for stability and a life where things stay the same for a while."

"You mean ..."

"I mean, perhaps you are both right. This may not be the right time for ECF to branch out and change, but you are right that one day it will need to. I believe there is a choice."

Tesfai knew the choice his wife saw before them: "Stay and argue, and maybe contribute to a split in the ECF, or resign and allow it to stay intact."

"Which would be the more loving thing to do?" Abeba's wise counsel continued. "If you resign, you need not turn your back on ECF; perhaps someday you will have a relationship again, in some other form. Remember the words of Ecclesiastes: 'To everything there is a season.' This may be the season for you to concentrate on studies here. And you still have your connection with Pastor Gibson and Mt. Olive church. You still have the support from the rest of the LCMS—people like Pastor Newton, Pastor Mengsteab, and Dr. Scudieri. All these people understand about missions and evangelizing!"

"Come to think of it, Pastor Gibson did say he wanted me as a part of Mt. Olive's ministry team once I complete my doctorate and return to San Jose."

"Tesfai, we've always put our fate into God's hands. Has God ever let us down? If ECF is not open to your vision of cross-cultural, cross-generational ministry, and if this is God's leading, then the opportunity will come along. God will provide!" Abeba spoke with confidence.

Tesfai repeated the Scripture his wife had quoted. "To everything there is a season. A time to plant, a time to reap. A time to mourn, a time to dance. Yes, I mourn that the ECF no longer feels it needs me. But I can also dance, for the confidence our new church, the LCMS, has placed in me."

Abeba began to sing, "Through many dangers, toils, and snares ..."

Tesfai joined quickly "We have already come. Tis grace that's brought us safe thus far, and grace will lead us home!"

Tesfai hugged his wife.

A BIG CHANGE

"So what happened after you got your doctorate?" asked Dr. Bob Scudieri, curiously. Tesfai and Bob were attending a mission gathering at Concordia Seminary in St. Louis. Bob, head of North American Missions for the LCMS, had taken a keen interest in Tesfai's progress. Like Pastors Newton and Mengsteab, he saw potential in Tesfai's approach to intergenerational outreach.

Pastor Tesfai smiled. "It wasn't easy, for Abeba or for me. I think even our sons, Abel and Daniel, wondered what was going to happen to us.

When the ECF rejected my vision, I was without a job.

"We had a tough year in 2006. Pastor Gibson welcomed me back to San Jose as a missionary on the Mt. Olive staff. Our idea was to foster a multi-ethnic worshipping group: seven or eight families, we hoped, would join the venture and be trained for outreach. Meanwhile, I would locate several Ethiopian families. Together we would plant a new church—one capable of cross-cultural ministry to reach the next generation."

Bob put his hand on Tesfai's shoulder. "That is a big need. It's not obvious to many Anglos in the church that we need to be missionaries. But many congregations are aware they have difficulty keeping their young people engaged. The problem might be helped by bringing together people from host churches and immigrant populations. Our young people are more used to being in a community that is diverse."

"That's what we figured. Pastor Gibson was enthusiastic. But then he got a call to pastor in southern California. He was a huge driver of this project. His leaving set us back. And then ..." Tesfai's voice trailed off. "I had not had health insurance while we were in Indiana, so when we returned to the Bay Area and got health coverage, I had a physical exam.

Just a routine, so I thought."

"It wasn't routine," guessed Bob.

"No. I was diagnosed with cancer. In fact, I got my cancer diagnosis about the same time that Mike got his call to southern California. I think Mike got the better deal.

"The rest of 2006 I had surgeries and recovery. God was gracious to us—I could have been diagnosed when I was without health insurance— and I am healed. But this meant I wasn't able to do anything about the Mt. Olive ministry until early 2007. But then the new pastor at Mt. Olive had a surprise for me."

"Surprise?"

"He was not interested in the vision Pastor Mike Gibson and I had shared. With me being gone during my cancer treatments, and with the lack of leadership interest at Mt. Olive, the whole thing fell apart. So there I was, a pastor at Mt. Olive, with no ministry. I pretty much had to start over. Mike and I had already settled on the name 'South Bay Mosaic Ministry', so I got permission to move this venture to First Immanuel Lutheran church in downtown San Jose, where Pastor Newton was involved. He was no longer pastor there, but since he was president of the LCMS's regional synod, he facilitated this move."

"How did that turn out?" asked Bob.

"It was interesting. Little of this new ministry had to do with Ethiopians. God seemed to be hinting at a different way for us to look at ministry. My call was to promote partnership between First Immanuel's English speaking members, which had been declining, and its Hispanic immigrant population which was healthier. I decided to start a Bible study and evangelize the student population at San Jose State University.

This would entail reaching young people of many cultures."

Bob wanted to hear more about the missionary's experience. "Tesfai, It sounds like you were doing a lot of running around," What did Abeba think about all of this? Did she get to see you at all?"

"Yes, but to be accurate, it was both of us doing the running around. We had fourteen or fifteen people, both Ethiopian and Caucasian, worshipping together, in English on Sunday afternoons. During the week, we had Bible studies at the university and home meetings. We were intent on supporting Christians in their faith walks as well as reaching nonbelievers.

We did this for nearly five years. I was hoping area LCMS churches would join. Two churches supported the work—First Immanuel, of course, and St. Mark's in Sunnyvale. They did assist with other kinds of support, including financial. Eventually, due to lack of personnel involvement in either outreach, and the fact that our people were far flung throughout the Bay Area, the Mosaic Ministry ended in 2010."

Bob expressed his sadness. "I hope this hasn't stopped you from using the things you learned."

"Abeba reminded me that when God calls, God provides. I did receive another call, which I accepted, to Bethesda Lutheran Communities in the Central Valley to minister to disabled adults. The people were wonderful, and I enjoyed my time with them, but still, my heart belonged to second-generation ministry. And the

Ethiopian population keeps growing. We figured God wouldn't bring us this far to let us go, so we waited."

"And?"

"God called us to go to an Ethiopian soccer tournament."

ADDIS KIDAN

"Soccer?" Bob looked quizzically at Tesfai. "Aren't you a bit old to be playing soccer at a tournament?"

"Not play, attend!" Tesfai laughed. "Abeba and I had kept in touch with the Ethiopian Christians. We often were asked to assist with outreach; it's just that none of these constituted a formal call to ministry. But then, there was this Ethiopian soccer tournament in San Jose in summer 2010. Ethiopian Christians in San Francisco saw it as a great place to evangelize, so they called us to do training for evangelists. We trained seventy volunteers who gave out 13,000 tracts about the love of Jesus."

"I didn't know there were that many Ethiopians in San Francisco," said Bob.

"They're from all over. They come into town for cultural and sporting events, then they return home. There were several Ethiopians living in San Francisco, though, who wanted to get a Bible study going. So, during the week I worked with Bethesda Lutheran Communities. On weekends Abeba and I went to San Francisco to help with the home Bible studies. Our connection and relationship matured and eventually this little group decided to plant a church in 2012. I had to discern: church planting in San

Francisco with Ethiopians or continue working with Bethesda? I couldn't do both anymore."

"You chose the church," remarked Bob.

"I did."

"That was risky."

"Abeba and I felt that church planting and evangelism were consistent with what we've always done. The LCMS agreed, and in 2013 I resigned from Bethesda and became a missionary at large within the Nevada/Hawai'i/California mission district. I have to thank Pastor Newton for this; it was through him I got this call."

"I can believe that. President Newton was a missionary overseas for many years. He knows what a mission field looks like. He knows that today the U.S. is one of the top mission fields."

"We named our new church Addis Kidan, which means New Covenant. We're immigrants, but we have children we want to encourage in the faith. Ethiopians and Eritreans have been successful immigrants in this country—we work hard, take education seriously, and do a lot to help one another. We don't take freedom for granted, including the freedom to practice our Christian faith. We look at Anglo Christians and wonder if they take Jesus as seriously as we do. Life can be easy here, comparatively speaking. So the new covenant includes us revitalizing the church wherever we can. This can be puzzling for lifelong, native born Christians, especially if they are white. It's strange for white people— including pastors—to think in terms of what immigrants can offer their church communities!"

"Addis Kidan represents a new covenant in many ways, not all of them obvious." Bob expressed pleasure in this new venture.

"Yes, you could say that. New Covenant: from one generation to the next; from one culture to another; from successful immigrants to people who are still struggling; from immigrant population to host population. When you have the convergence of all these groups, they enrich one another and become a real Christian community."

Bob listened and smiled. "This sounds like what John describes as the population of heaven: many different ethnic groups, from many parts of the world. All coming together, one in Christ."

"After being in a couple of neighborhoods, meeting in people's homes, it turns out we can also be a new covenant for a historic church in San Francisco! That church, Bethel, had been ministering in San Francisco for over ninety years—until ten years ago. At some point, the remaining members could no longer afford to keep the building functioning.

"These fine people ended up going to another church, Christ for All Nations, but they never forgot the people here. And the people in the neighborhood, many of them immigrants living alongside native born Caucasians and African-Americans, never forgot the good that Bethel had accomplished."

"So?" Bob was clearly intrigued.

"I learned the building was vacant and made inquiries. In 2014 we began occupying the building. It's taken hard work, and I can't begin to tell you all the people who have helped us financially, but here we are. We have a place to meet and now we are looking at next steps." Tesfai was talking quickly.

"Next steps? Tesfai, what has God put on your heart?"

"We are thrilled to be able to meet in the Bethel location. And we discovered that the neighbors—maybe 75,000 people—are happy to have the building open and ministry functioning again. Some of them have even stopped by the church to tell us this! This seemed to be an invitation, and we began to ask, 'Are we supposed to come here, worship on Sunday, and then just go home until the next Sunday?' Remember, the nucleus of Addis Kidan doesn't live in the neighborhood. Our Ethiopian service is in Amharic, which is good for us, but not good for anyone else hungry to hear about the love of Jesus. Nor for our youth."

"Which means ..."

"We decided to be intentional about ministry to the neighborhood. Thanks to our younger members—including, I am happy to say, my second son Daniel—we've got an English language youth service on Sunday morning. So not only do we make ourselves accessible to the neighbors, we also involve the youth! We started a Friday evening youth program. We've got a Thursday evening English gathering which targets a wider range of ages. There is a good chance that the various English services will merge, and we will have planted a new church—one with an English name! I tell you, Bob, the neighborhood has responded to our outreach with great joy!"

Bob sat back to take this in. This new immigrant church was succeeding where many don't. And it saw itself as a mission to its multi-ethnic neighborhood. "This is wonderful! The outreach and enthusiasm you are experiencing is moving even for me. It's also a little different, immigrants reaching out to nonimmigrants."

"Yes. Here we are, an immigrant church, starting an English-speaking church for those who are not Ethiopians, though of course Ethiopians can attend, and may well do so," declared Tesfai. "We don't want to just give some space to a church made up of people from the surrounding community, we are planning to give full support to a new cross-cultural, intergenerational church!" Tesfai was becoming increasingly ebullient.

"It turns out that ministering to the needs of second-generation Ethiopians can be translated to other populations. First, though, we have to make sure the kids are engaged. We cannot allow our young people to feel left out!"

"God has done amazing things with you!" Bob thought back on all he knew about Tesfai's journey. "God picked you from the time you were in Ethiopia, shaped you for ministry during your time in Saudi Arabia and Sudan, and then brought you to us. You are a gift from God."

"It's not about me!" Tesfai objected to the implication. "It's about serving God, Who took an imperfect man and used various accidents to make him into a witness to Jesus's love. Thanks to Abeba, I have seen that there is a plan, and I am part of it. Thanks to my sons, I have come to realize the needs of the second generation of immigrants."

Bob agreed. "The Lord who planned to bring His Son from heaven to earth, did not find it strange to bring a non-believer from Africa, shape and form him in countries hostile to Christianity, all to bring His love to young people in America."

Tesfai became reflective. "You know Bob, there are some who think it was an accident that I became a Christian, and that I now serve as a missionary to America. I don't believe it. There are only women and men sent by God, according to His plan to love the world. His plan existed since the beginning of the universe. His love is no accident, and there are no accidental missionaries."

Made in the USA
Columbia, SC
24 February 2018